PENGUIN HANDBOOKS

PH37

ROSES

F. FAIRBROTHER

This is the first of a series of gardening hand-books to be published by Penguin Books in co-operation with The Royal Horticultural Society. The editor of the series is the editor of their publications, Patrick M. Synge. The book is a practical manual for all who would like to grow roses. It contains plans for rose gardens and details of preparing the soil, planting, cultivation, pruning, propagating, and preparing roses for show. Each point is fully illustrated by photographs in the text and there is also a descriptive list of over 200 rose varieties with photographs of most of the noted ones and interesting chapters on the history of the rose and on shrub roses.

The Queen Elizabeth Rose

ROSES

F. FAIRBROTHER

*Prepared in conjunction and collaboration
with The Royal Horticultural Society*

PENGUIN BOOKS

Penguin Books Ltd, Harmondsworth, Middlesex
U.S.A.: Penguin Books Inc., 3300 Clipper Mill Road, Baltimore 11, Md
AUSTRALIA: Penguin Books Pty Ltd, 762 Whitehorse Road,
Mitcham, Victoria

—

First published 1958
Reprinted with revisions 1958

—

Made and printed in Great Britain by
Jarrold & Sons Ltd, Norwich

CONTENTS

LIST OF PLATES

Double Digging

Planting and Pruning Rose Trees

Pruning of a Standard Rose Tree, Hybrid Tea Type

LIST OF PLATES

Pruning of Floribunda Roses

Pruning of Ramblers

LIST OF PLATES

Pruning Roses Under Glass

Shrub Roses

Exhibiting

Selected Roses

LIST OF TEXT FIGURES

FOREWORD

THIS is the first of this series of gardening books in whose publication The Royal Horticultural Society and Penguin Books have collaborated, and I am glad to welcome its appearance. We hope that this series may help many gardeners, particularly those who are just starting with small gardens around new houses, and so we have planned a number of titles. The books, although written by experts, have been kept as simple as possible and there are many pictures.

It is also fitting that a book on roses should be the first to appear in the new series, for roses are so particularly our national flower and are surely as widely grown as any flower in this country. There is great variety in roses, including the Hybrid Tea roses with large and perfectly modelled blooms; the shrub roses with looser habit and smaller flowers, a form of rose which is especially suitable for modern labour-saving gardens; the Floribunda roses which keep up a display throughout a very long season; and finally the old roses of our forefathers, which have recently come back into popularity and are proving again such good garden plants. We should not neglect the species roses, some of which are of incomparable loveliness and the majority of which are easy to grow. These are the earliest of roses to flower, and by growing them in addition to the other types mentioned we can have roses flowering from early May until the end of October. So roses are indeed good plants for the small garden. They are also tough plants which are difficult to kill, while on the other hand they yield great returns to the keen gardener who will give them his best attention and care.

Mr Fairbrother has been a rose enthusiast all his life and has been a Vice-President of the National Rose Society for a number of years. He has already been selected as its next President and will take office in 1959, and I venture to think that no more appropriate choice could have been made for the authorship of this book.

D. BOWES-LYON
President, The Royal Horticultural Society

AUTHOR'S PREFACE AND
ACKNOWLEDGEMENTS

IN writing this book on Roses it has been my object to interest the beginner as well as the more experienced in rose culture. The various operations are described in simple language and the illustrations should help in the understanding of the text. The descriptive list of roses will be a guide in the selection of trees either for replacement or for the completely new rose garden.

I am indebted to Mr Edland, Secretary of the National Rose Society for helpful suggestions, to Mr Baines at the N.R.S. Trial Grounds for assistance given when photographs were being taken, to Mr J. E. Downward who not only provided the majority of the photographs but took great pains in the selection of the material, to Miss D. Sibeth for the original drawings to illustrate budding, to the Director of the Victoria and Albert Museum for some of the illustrations in Chapter 1, to Alex Dickson and Sons for permission to use a coloured illustration of 'Shepherd's Delight' on the cover, to John Sanday (Roses Ltd) for the photograph used in Plate 89, to Messrs Wheatcroft Brothers for the table giving the ancestry of 'The Queen Elizabeth' rose, to *The Times* for the photograph on p. 45, to the Shell Photographic Unit for Plates 63, 65, 66, 68 and 69, to Professor T. Wallace, F.R.S., for Plates 57–61, to Mrs D. C. Stemler, Will Tillotson's Roses, California, for Plate 13, and to Mr Patrick M. Synge for most helpful constructive criticism during the compilation of the book.

To all I record my most grateful thanks.

CHAPTER I

THE ANCESTRY OF OUR MODERN ROSES

Oh! no man knows
Through what wild centuries
Roves back the rose.

WALTER DE LA MARE

As one looks at a bed of modern roses one rarely realizes the fascinating history which lies hidden in them. They represent years of patient hybridizing and careful selection on the part of many good rosarians. Their life story carries us back into the remote ages, for the rose in some form or another has been growing on this earth for millions of years. It is older than man himself and fossils of the rose, said to be more than thirty million years old, have been found in Oregon and in Colorado.

The rose has figured in the mythology of ancient civilizations; poets of almost every nation have sung its praises, artists have been inspired by it and have used it in various ways. It is found as a motif in architectural decoration, in jewellery, in pottery, and in embroidery. In ritual, too, its associations have been happy ones. Wherever it has grown it has quickly found its way into human hearts.

Probably the earliest use of the rose in design in European countries is seen in the Minoan period (2800–1900 B.C.). Minoan goldsmiths excelled in their reproductions of flowers and foliage; gold pins terminating in heads representing wide-open, single roses have been found in the Mochlos tombs in Crete. Decorative rose sprays are found on chalices as early as 1600 B.C. One of the earliest known illustrations of the rose in

1. Part of a fresco at Knossos, Crete, showing a six-petalled rose

decoration was found in the House of Frescoes at Knossos, Crete, and dates from about the middle of the sixteenth century B.C. An illustration of a portion of one of these frescoes is shown in Plate 1. It is interesting to note the flowers have six petals instead of five, but the leaves are obviously those of the rose.

The island of Rhodes in the eastern Mediterranean was given its name from the Greek *rhodon* (rose), thus commemorating the rose which flourished profusely in that island. So far as is known the only representation of a rose dating from the days of Ancient Greece is on coins in the island of Rhodes. There are, however, frequent references to the rose in Greek poetry and in Greek mythology. Probably the earliest poem in praise of the rose was written by Anacreon in the fifth century B.C.

> *The rose is the perfume of the Gods, the joy of men,*
> *It adorns the Graces at the blossoming of Love*
> *It is the favoured flower of Venus.*

Homer in the *Iliad* referred to the rose as the source of perfume for the oil with which Aphrodite anointed the dead Hector. The rose was also used by the Greeks for garlands at feasts, a custom developed to a much greater extent at a later date by the Romans.

In classical times roses were found growing wild in all the countries of the eastern Mediterranean. Some were single roses with five petals and others are recorded as having up to one hundred petals. It is difficult to say with truth how the double roses developed from the single

2. *R. gallica*, pink and red forms

roses, but it is highly probable that at some stage in their growth the wild roses threw out 'sports' which bore double flowers and the ever-watchful gardener selected these for further propagation. Herodotus, the Greek historian, gives the first account of a double rose: 'They (the Greeks) then coming to another district of Macedonia, settled near the gardens of Midas in which wild roses grew, each one having sixty leaves (petals) surpassing all other known roses in fragrance.' The identity of this double rose is not known with certainty, but it is highly probable that it was a double form of *Rosa damascena* (Plate 5), the sweet-scented damask rose. This rose was descended from *R. gallica* (the red rose or *R. rubra*) and was one of the parents of our modern roses (Plates 2 and 3).

R. gallica, from which is derived in part the dark red of our modern roses, is of very ancient origin; known to the Persians in the twelfth century B.C., it probably reached Italy and France during the Persian invasion of the West. The autumn damask rose may have been the rose described by the Roman encyclopaedist, Pliny, as *Praeneste*, which he said flowered latest of all and certainly was the twice-flowering Rose of Paestum mentioned by Virgil. This rose was the result of a cross between *R. gallica* and *R. moschata* (a native of western Asia and of China) (Plates 4, 6). Two other roses growing in the Mediterranean countries which were destined to have an influence in the development of our garden roses were *R. phoenicea*, a straggling bush with single white flowers, and our own native dog briar *R. canina*, well known in our hedgerows today. The four species (*R. gallica*, *R. moschata*, *R. phoenicea*, *R. canina*) were known in the fourth century B.C., and the garden roses of Greek and Roman times were produced by crossing and re-crossing these species.

The Romans were extravagant in the use of the rose at their feasts. Whether these were banquets to celebrate their victories, or meetings of a more confidential type,

3. *R. gallica*, from a painting by Alfred Parsons, R.A., in *The Genus Rosa*, by Ellen Willmott

the rose was present in abundance. The Roman warriors were crowned with garlands of roses, the food at their feasts was decorated with rose petals, and frequently the fragrant oil obtained from the rose was sprinkled on it. After-dinner gossip among heads garlanded with roses was treated with the respect of diplomatic conversations and regarded as confidential. It is to this practice that we owe the derivation of the term *sub rosa*. The Romans were good gardeners, and by them the rose was extensively

4. *R. moschata*

5. *R. damascena* 'Omar Khayyám', the rose from Omar Khayyám's tomb in Persia, which has also been planted on Edward Fitzgerald's grave in Suffolk. The flowers are pink

6. *R. moschata* in China, from a photograph taken by the famous plant collector G. Forrest

7. Young Prince with a rose, from a sixteenth-century Persian miniature

8. Brocaded satin showing a rose from a seventeenth-century Persian embroidery

cultivated and the demand for roses was always great. They undoubtedly brought many roses to this country during the period of the Roman occupation.

The next important influence on the spread of the rose throughout the world was due to the advance of Islam. When the Arabs conquered Persia they came to a land where flowers were loved, and as their empire extended from Spain in the west to India in the east these flowers, including the rose, followed them.

The rose was frequently used by the Persians in their designs. It was used as a decorative motif on porcelain and was woven into their tapestries and carpets. It is to the Persians that we are indebted for the double yellow *R. hemisphaerica* (the Sulphur rose) which came to the countries of modern Europe by way of Austria. It was introduced into England in the early years of the seventeenth century, but it seldom opened in our climate, and

23

9. An English embroidery of the seventeenth century showing the
rose with some of its pests

so was of little use to the hybridists who wished to use it
to introduce yellow into our then known roses. It was not
until much later (1837) that this became possible by the
introduction of *R. foetida persiana* (the Persian Yellow), a
double rose, and *R. foetida* (*R. lutea*), the Austrian briar,
a single yellow rose. Their influence on our modern roses
is dealt with later (p. 30).

Prior to this, a great advance had been made by the
introduction into this country, at some time in the latter
half of the eighteenth century, of roses from China and
Burma. Two of these, *R. chinensis* (crimson China) and
R. gigantea, the wild tea rose of Burma, and crosses of
them, were perpetual flowering but unfortunately were
not robust enough to flourish out of doors in our English
climate except in the more sheltered gardens of the south.
They were more suited to the climate of France and Italy
to which countries they were introduced in the first years
of the nineteenth century.

10. *R. chinensis* from a drawing by Alfred Parsons, R.A., in *The Genus Rosa* by Ellen Willmott

It is generally accepted that there are about 120 different species found in various parts of the Northern Hemisphere. Some of these are referred to in the chapter on shrub roses, but cannot be dealt with fully in a book of this size. In this chapter the history of seven main species only has been traced (*R. gallica, R. phoenicea, R. moschata, R. canina, R. chinensis, R. gigantea,* and *R. lutea*). These were the ancestors of the many types of roses which flourished in English gardens towards the end of the nineteenth century; we now turn to examine the classes which have been developed from these species.

Hybrid Perpetuals

The influence of the China roses on the established roses of that time was great indeed and marked the first real advance in rose culture. The Crimson China (*R. chinensis*) was crossed and recrossed with *R. gigantea,* and gave rise to a number of hybrid China roses which were perpetual flowering. These were used in England and in France for hybridizing with the Autumn Damask (*R. damascena bifera*), the object being to produce roses which flowered more than once in the season and yet had greater substance and a stronger constitution than the China roses. It must be remembered that prior to about A.D. 1800 roses in this country and in Europe flowered only once in a season with the exception of *R. damascena bifera*. The roses had a short season, just as other flowering shrubs, and flowered only in June or July. The line 'Gather ye rose buds while ye may' loses its urgency today when one can gather rosebuds almost all the year round, but in the days of Robert Herrick (1597–1674) the reference was particularly apposite.

An important cross worthy of special mention was one between 'Parson's Pink China' (one of the *R. chinensis* × *R. gigantea* crosses) and the Pink Autumn Damask. This produced the first of a class known as the Bourbon roses. It was produced in 1817 in the French island of Bourbon in the southern Indian Ocean. The Bourbons and another

11. A fine specimen of a Bourbon rose, 'Mme Lauriol de Barney'

cross between the China rose and *R. damascena bifera*, the Portland rose, were highly scented and generally flowered in the autumn as well as in the summer. They were in fact the Hybrid Perpetuals in embryo, and further crossings of them with the hybrid Chinas increased the size and quality of the blooms and ensured more continuous flowering.

During the last decade of the eighteenth century the Empress Josephine established her famous rose garden at the Palace of Malmaison near Paris. Here were assembled representative roses from all parts of the world; seeds were collected from natural crossings and the best seedlings were retained for future breeding. It was in no small measure due to this lively patronage that the Hybrid Perpetuals were developed and improved. The Roseraie de l'Häy and the Bagatelle gardens now take the place of the former famous rose garden at Malmaison.

For fifty years, from 1840 to 1890, the Hybrid Perpetuals were firm favourites in our English gardens. They were robust and thrived in our island climate, many of them were highly scented and some flowered a second time in the same season. Some of the Hybrid Perpetuals are still to be found in our gardens, roses such as 'General Jacqueminot', 'Mrs John Laing', 'Ulrich Brunner', 'Frau Karl Druschki', 'George Dickson', 'Hugh Dickson', all of which have been favourites over a long period of time and which have a following today. It is over a century since 'General Jacqueminot' was first introduced and it is still worth growing if only for its scent.

The Tea Roses

These roses are supposed to owe their name to a similarity in scent to that of the China tea chests which were commonly imported into England during the Victorian era. The scent is certainly very delicate and is probably due partly to the influence of the Musk rose (*R. moschata*) in its ancestry. The first Tea rose, which was pink, was

12. A Hybrid Perpetual rose, 'Frau Karl Druschki'

raised in France as a result of a cross between the Blush Tea Scented China and one of the Bourbons.

The crossing of the Musk rose with 'Parson's Pink China' gave rise to the Noisette rose, which combined the climbing habit and scent of the former with the semi-double pink flowers of the latter. In the years 1820–30 the Noisette rose was a great favourite.

It was when attempting to produce a yellow Noisette by crossing the pink Noisette with the yellow China (another of the crosses *R. chinensis* × *R. gigantea*) that a yellow rose was produced which was more typically a Tea rose than a Noisette. When this yellow Noisette-Tea was recrossed with the Yellow China in 1838 the creamy-white, sweetly fragrant Tea rose, 'Devoniensis', was produced.

Thus both Pink and Yellow Tea roses were available for crossing, and these crosses produced that most exquisite family of Tea roses so much loved in the latter half of the nineteenth century. These roses had a distinctively sweet scent, a beautiful form, and delicate colouring, but

29

unfortunately they were not robust. Few of them would grow out of doors except in the most sheltered and sunny gardens. It was under glass that their beauty was fully revealed. A conservatory containing well-grown specimens of 'Niphetos' (white), 'Maman Cochet' (pale rose), 'Madame Hoste' (yellow) is a sight never to be forgotten. More vigorous (because nearer the Noisette type) are 'Maréchal Niel' and that grand old favourite 'Gloire de Dijon', which, in spite of its being introduced more than one hundred years ago, still clothes the walls of old cottages and fills the air with its delicious fragrance.

Hybrid Teas

It will be obvious to all who have read this chapter that the crossing of the vigorous but generally badly shaped Hybrid Perpetuals with the more delicate but well-formed Teas was inevitable. In fact, the first of a new class, the Hybrid Teas, was produced in 1867 – that well-loved rose 'La France'. The Hybrid Teas quickly caught the attention of rose growers, and it was recognized that here was a class which had the good qualities of both the Hybrid Perpetuals and the Teas. It was not until 1884 that the new group was recognized as distinct from the Hybrid Perpetuals. Some of the earlier ones, such as 'Madame Abel Chatenay' and 'Caroline Testout', are still with us and are enchantingly lovely.

In the year 1900 when Pernet-Ducher produced that striking yellow rose 'Soleil d'Or' we entered an almost breath-taking period in the history of the Hybrid Tea roses. Here was the opportunity hybridists had awaited with eagerness. The Persian Yellow, *R. foetida* (*R. lutea*) was to be the means of introducing a richness and range of colour hitherto unknown in our rose gardens. Pernet-Ducher had crossed the Persian Yellow with Hybrid Perpetuals, and after several years of patient work produced 'Soleil d'Or'. No one could have foretold the wealth of colour which this introduction was to give to the Hybrid Tea roses. All the shades from yellow through

13. The first Hybrid Tea rose, 'La France'

apricot to deep orange and orange tinged with pink or scarlet were to result from crossing the Pernet roses with the Hybrid Teas. Unfortunately the joy of the brilliant colours was tempered by the troubles which other characteristics of the Persian Yellow were to bring to our roses. In the early stages the delicious scent which the Hybrid Teas had inherited from their ancestors was lost. Other weaknesses of *R. foetida* were susceptibility to black spot and die-back. For a time rose enthusiasts tried to persuade themselves that colour and form were more important than scent; but there is no gainsaying the fact that the first thing anyone does when handed a rose is to smell it!

By careful breeding the scent has been largely restored in some of our newest roses to a remarkable degree. The weak constitution and liability to black spot are much more difficult to eradicate, but careful hybridizing can do and is doing much.

31

Hybrid Polyantha Climbers, Poly Pompons, Floribundas, and Ramblers

About the middle of the nineteenth century *R. multiflora* was introduced from China and Japan. This species gave rise to two classes of roses, first a class of hybrid polyantha climbers, such as 'Paul's Scarlet Climber' and 'Chaplin's Pink', and secondly dwarf seedlings which, when crossed with the China roses, produced the class known as Poly Pompons. These dwarf roses produced the ever-blooming quality of the China roses and the huge clusters of *R. multiflora*. The earliest of the Poly Pompons were given the charming names of 'Pâquerette' (white) and 'Mignonette' (pink). The latter became the ancestor of other well-known members of this group, the Orlean's rose, 'Edith Cavell', and 'Coral Cluster'. The Poly Pompons are charming little plants and may be used as edgings to the beds of the larger Hybrid Teas. They also make most attractive half standards, and as such may be used in the foreground of the shrub garden.

In 1924 Svend Poulsen of Denmark began to cross the Poly Pompons with the Hybrid Teas and produced a completely new class, the members of which were originally called Hybrid Polyanthas and now are called Floribundas. The group which started with the Poulsen roses, 'Else Poulsen' and 'Kirsten Poulsen', soon included 'Karen Poulsen', 'Anne Poulsen', 'Poulsen's Copper', 'Poulsen's Pink', 'Poulsen's Bedder', and others. At the present time the Floribundas are amongst the most popular of our roses and include such well-known varieties as 'Frensham', 'Masquerade', 'Dainty Maid', 'Orange Triumph', 'Moulin Rouge', 'Red Favourite', 'Concerto', 'Korona', and 'The Queen Elizabeth' rose. They are comparatively easy to grow, are disease-resistant, and give a good display of colourful blooms from early June to December. Many make excellent hedges, and all are good for massing in a rose border.

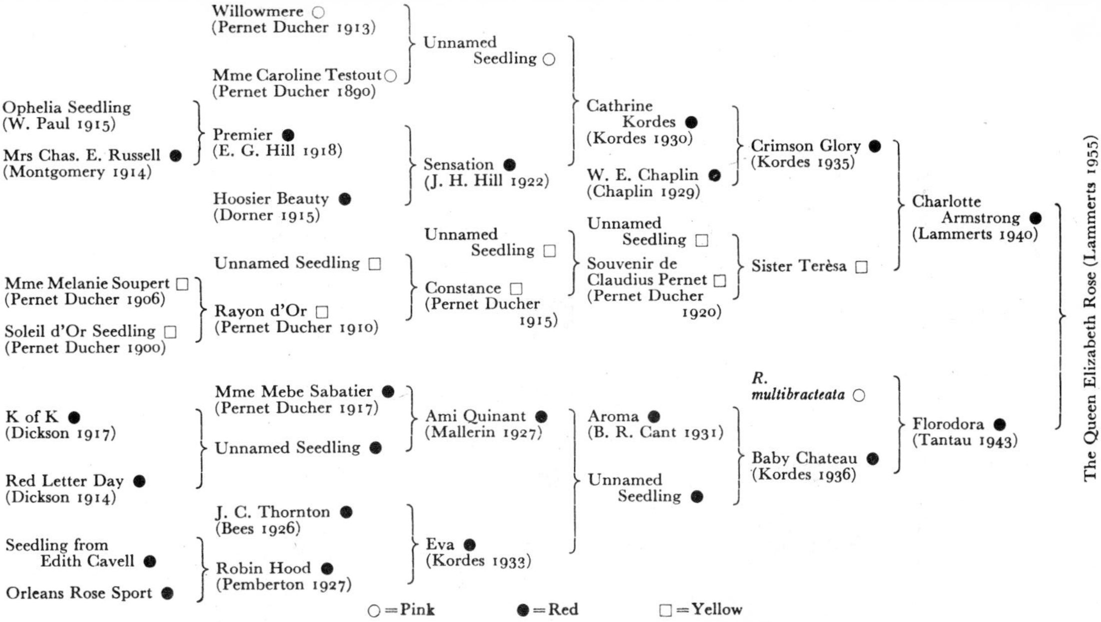

Figure 1. The ancestry of 'The Queen Elizabeth' Rose

The Queen Elizabeth Rose (Lammerts 1935)

Charlotte Armstrong (Lammerts 1940)

Crimson Glory (Kordes 1935)

Florodora (Tantau 1943)

Cathrine Kordes (Kordes 1930)

W. E. Chaplin (Chaplin 1929)

Sister Teresa □

R. multibracteata ○

Baby Chateau (Kordes 1936)

Unnamed Seedling ○

Sensation (J. H. Hill 1922)

Unnamed Seedling □

Souvenir de Claudius Pernet (Pernet Ducher 1920)

Aroma (B. R. Cant 1931)

Unnamed Seedling

Willowmere (Pernet Ducher 1913)

Mme Caroline Testout ○ (Pernet Ducher 1890)

Premier (E. G. Hill 1918)

Hoosier Beauty (Dorner 1915)

Unnamed Seedling □

Constance □ (Pernet Ducher 1915)

Ami Quinant (Mallerin 1927)

Unnamed Seedling

Eva (Kordes 1933)

Ophelia Seedling (W. Paul 1915)

Mrs Chas. E. Russell (Montgomery 1914)

Mme Melanie Soupert □ (Pernet Ducher 1906)

Soleil d'Or Seedling □ (Pernet Ducher 1910)

Rayon d'Or □ (Pernet Ducher 1910)

Mme Mebe Sabatier (Pernet Ducher 1917)

Unnamed Seedling

J. C. Thornton (Bees 1926)

Robin Hood (Pemberton 1927)

K of K (Dickson 1917)

Red Letter Day (Dickson 1914)

Seedling from Edith Cavell

Orleans Rose Sport

○ = Pink   ● = Red   □ = Yellow

B   33

14. Bed of the Floribunda rose 'Queen Elizabeth' in the Queen Mary Rose Garden, Regent's Park, London

Soon after the introduction of *R. multiflora* another rose species of rambling habit was introduced from Japan. It was *R. wichuraiana*. This and its crosses with *R. multiflora* and with the Hybrid Teas produced the well-known Ramblers 'Excelsa', 'Albertine', 'Alberic Barbier', 'Dorothy Perkins', 'American Pillar', and others of similar type. These used to be, and in many gardens still are, very popular for covering rustic screens and pergolas. Strong favourites are, however, the climbing sports of the Hybrid Teas, which not only have great covering capacity but also carry the beautiful Hybrid Tea blooms.

The most recent type of Climbers, the Kordesii Climbers, which bloom all the way up trees, bid fair to supplant the Climbing Sports as favourites.

And so the hybridists' work goes on, the quest for the perfect rose continues. Who knows what the future has in store, blue roses perhaps, or maybe thornless roses. With the latter achievement Milton's picture of the Paradisal Rose will be realized: 'Flowers of all hue, and without thorn the rose.'

CHAPTER 2

PLANNING THE ROSE GARDEN

The design of the rose garden is largely determined for many of us by the size of the plot of ground available. It may be so small that not more than one bed about twelve feet six inches by five feet can be devoted to roses. In this event it would be advisable to grow only Hybrid Teas. It would certainly be a start, and a bed of this size would take twenty-four trees arranged in three rows of eight. If there is freedom of choice, select an open space free from overhanging trees and where the sun shines on the bed most of the day. A little shade from the midday sun will be welcome during the summer months, but wherever the bed is placed the soil must be well drained, for nothing so shortens the life of a rose tree as water-logged soil.

It may be that the land at your disposal will enable you to be a little more ambitious. Possibly you may be able to make several rose beds. If so, how will you arrange them?

The design of a rose garden is so personal a matter that one hesitates even to make suggestions. The rose lover will wish to have certain conditions fulfilled. He will wish to be able to plant, prune, and tend his trees without too much trampling on the soil. He will wish the design to be such as to reveal the full beauty of the roses both to himself and to his friends. He may wish to see all the roses at one glance, standing say on a terrace and looking over the whole garden, or he may wish to hide part from view and so provide a surprise round the corner. He will certainly wish to limit the work entailed in edging if the paths are of grass – and nothing enhances the beauty of rose blooms so much as well-kept grass paths round the beds – so he will wish to avoid a large number of small beds.

In the Victorian era the design of rose gardens was extremely formal, and the result looked rather like a complicated geometrical figure, very symmetrical and often very dull. There were many small beds, usually edged with dwarf box hedges kept carefully clipped, about nine inches high, and there was the inevitable sundial as the centrepiece. Such a rose-garden design is rather fussy and requires too much laborious maintenance for present-day conditions. It is quite true that rectangular beds are the easiest to work and rectangular paths the easiest to mow, but their use is almost bound to make the design somewhat formal. The illustrations given in Figure 2a and Figure 2b suggest two ways of treating a small rose garden, say twenty feet by thirty feet. Figure 2a gives simple bold treatment, using three long

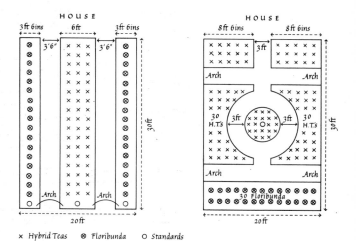

× Hybrid Teas   ⊗ Floribunda   O Standards

Figure 2a. A simple but bold treatment for a small garden

Figure 2b. The same area as 2a arranged to break the monotony of rectangular beds

15. Scarlet fruits of *R. rugosa*

rectangular beds, one six feet wide taking some sixty Hybrid Tea roses, and two narrower, three feet six inches wide arranged parallel to the first bed. These narrower beds may be used for Floribunda roses and will take about twenty trees in each bed. All the beds can be cultivated without trampling on the soil, and the grass paths are easily mown. The simple design is quite effective as the flanking beds of Floribundas act as a protective boundary to the bed of Hybrid Teas. If so desired three standards or half standards may be planted, one in each bed, at the end remote from the house. Also arches may be constructed at the same end linking the beds together and carrying ramblers or climbing sports.

Figure 2b shows the same area arranged to break the monotony of the rectangular beds. The centre circular bed is flanked by two rectangular beds with semicircles cut out of the two sides facing the centre. The rectangular beds at the end near the house lie on each side of a centre path, while the one at the other end occupies the full width of the garden. A standard or half-standard rose tree may be planted in the centre of the circular bed, and

37

Hybrid Tea rose trees planted in concentric circles round it.

Figure 3 shows a possible layout of a rose garden forty-five feet by thirty feet. This design combines the rectangular beds with a less formal portion. It permits of 'surprises', cutting off, by a rose hedge of Floribundas or Hybrid Musks, some of the beds containing the Hybrid Teas and also some of the old-fashioned shrub roses. As many of the shrub roses will have finished blooming in July a border of Poly Pompons may be planted to give colour during August and September before the berries ripen on the shrub roses. The two beds containing the shrub roses can be planted with early and late daffodils, with grape hyacinths, scillas, snowdrops, and crocuses so that colour will be given during February, March, April, and May before the roses bloom. As the shrub roses do

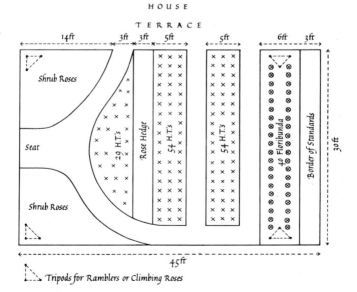

Figure 3. Suggested layout of a rose garden 45 feet by 30 feet

16. Orange-scarlet fruits of *R. moyesii*

not require such cultural operations as the Hybrid Teas, the bulbs are not a hindrance to subsequent cultivation.

In addition to providing accommodation for a representative collection of Hybrid Teas, Floribundas, Hybrid Musks, and shrub roses, provision is made for four tripods, along the sides of which ramblers or climbing sports may be trained.

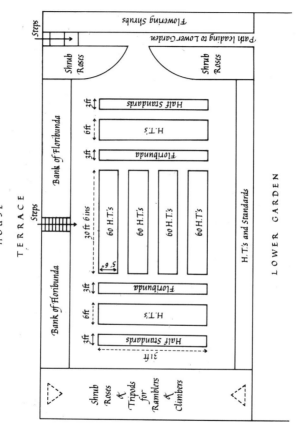

Figure 4. The author's rose garden. Adaptation of an old tennis court

Figure 4 shows a suggested adaptation of a grass tennis court or large lawn. If this is surrounded by banks rising not too steeply from the lawn so much the better, for these can be utilized for planting masses of Floribundas and arranging some of the fine shrub roses, which are again becoming popular, either as specimen bushes or for massed effect. The haunting perfume of many of the shrub roses fills the air in June, and the red hips enhance the garden in the autumn. The masses of Floribundas give an almost breath-taking colour effect during their long flowering period from June until the winter frosts end their brilliant display.

The arrangement of four beds, each thirty feet six inches by five feet six inches, parallel to the terrace and flanked on each side by three beds of varying widths, breaks the monotony of the rectangular beds. The paths between the beds are all three feet wide, and the mowing is easy, as one can get a good straight run for the machine. The grass border enclosing the beds is much wider, seven to eight feet, and allows for sitting space in the garden.

This plan provides room for a fairly representative collection of roses, some four hundred and fifty Hybrid Teas, a hundred Floribundas, twenty or thirty shrub roses, a dozen or so standards (or half standards), and several specimens of Ramblers and Climbers covering arches or trained on tripods. The effect produced is most pleasing and when the roses are in bloom the garden is a joy to behold. The variety of bulbs planted in the shrub borders, together with such dwarf plants as *Primula* 'Wanda' or various polyanthuses used as edgings to the larger beds, provide a gaiety of colour during the weeks of spring and do not interfere with later cultural operations. ·

A row or two of the more floriferous or more highly scented Hybrid Tea roses may be grown in the kitchen garden, specifically for cutting for the house.

These are a few suggestions which may help in planning the layout of your rose garden, but the detailed

17. Deep red fruits of *R. rubrifolia*

arrangement must remain your own personal affair. There is nothing quite so fascinating as planning and developing your own garden and no labour so rewarding as that entailed in the making of it.

In the more spacious days before the First World War large estates could devote considerable space to rose

18. Corner of the Queen Mary Rose Garden in Regent's Park, London

gardens, pergolas, arches, colonnades, and the like and the owners could afford to keep gardeners to attend them. Nowadays the small garden with the owner gardener is

19. The Queen Mary Rose Garden, Regent's Park. General view

the order of the day, and larger gardens are left to municipal authorities to lay out in their parks. The rose has taken its place in such gardens and also on low double walls which sometimes divide the dual carriageways of our wider roads. The Floribundas lend themselves admirably to such use, and also to the clothing of the often so desolate roundabouts on our main arterial roads. I have seen the V formed by the junction of two roads filled with the Floribunda 'Frensham', and a truly lovely sight it was, and this was in an industrial town in the north of England.

Cities and towns as well as sea-side resorts have taken up the idea of floral beds and small parks, and have done much to satisfy the longing for flowers in those who are compelled to live without a garden of their own. The National Rose Society of Great Britain some years ago created a Rose Garden in Regent's Park. The late Queen Mary who was patron of the Society at the time and who was a great lover of the rose, gave her gracious consent to its being named The Queen Mary Rose Garden. The photographs (Plates 18 and 19) give some idea of the beauty of this garden, and visitors to London in July or September should not fail to see it.

The long period of blooming of the rose in public gardens is illustrated by the photograph (Plate 20) of a bed of 'Peace' in St James's Park, London, which was printed in *The Times* on 31 December 1955.

Municipal authorities are to be congratulated on the work they have done to remove the drab effect of the Victorian era in our industrial towns and cities, and may rest assured their efforts are greatly appreciated by those who live in the towns and those who pass through them.

20. Rose 'Peace' in bloom in St James's Park on 31 December 1955

45

CHAPTER 3

PREPARATION OF THE ROSE BEDS

T HE initial preparation of the rose beds depends to a certain extent on the type of soil present in the garden. It is not possible to give a detailed account of soils in this book, but a few considerations may be useful regarding the physical properties of two extremes of soils: clay soils and sand or gravel soils.

CLAY SOILS are fine grained and capillarity will thus cause a lifting of water from the general water-table level below the surface of the soil. This factor alone would be an advantage in a dry season, but unfortunately in the fine-grained clay there is high surface tension, and the water is held so tenaciously that it is more difficult for the root hairs to extract the moisture. This type of soil therefore tends to become waterlogged and needs careful drainage. Another physical property of clay soils is the tendency to surface caking. This is particularly noticeable when the sun shines on the soil after rain. Surface caking leads to rapid evaporation of the surface water, and this causes cooling of the soil. Clay soils therefore take longer to reach the optimum temperature for plant growth than do other soils.

SAND AND GRAVEL SOILS on the other hand are coarse grained. The general water-table level is considerably lower as there is little or no capillarity. Surface tension is very much less, and therefore water is not held in spaces between the particles but quickly drains away. There is no caking of the surface, and surface water therefore is not evaporated but immediately passes to the lower level of soil. Such a soil tends to become dry and hot. Any rain falling on this type of soil is easily available to the root hairs because of the low surface tension, but unfortunately the water drains away so rapidly that frequent overhead irrigation is necessary to prevent drying out.

The best type of soil from a physical structure point of view is that which is fine grained enough to possess considerable surface, thus being capable of holding water by surface tension and yet coarse grained enough to allow good drainage. If you are fortunate enough to have a garden made on a piece of ground which has recently been good meadow land, and the texture is such that when you enclose some of the soil in your hand it does not immediately fall to powder when you release the pressure but breaks up on rubbing you may rest assured that it is good soil for roses.

More often than not one has to use land which has been growing crops for some years, and while such soil is easy to dig it lacks body and will require considerable addition of plant food.

Whatever type of soil you have to deal with some preliminary preparation of the beds is necessary. There are two extreme schools of thought regarding their preparation. One extreme advocates deep trenching, even to a depth of three feet, while the other advocates no digging at all, but advises planting the rose trees on the top of the bed and covering the roots with heaps of soil and compost. Advocates of both these methods claim excellent results, and under certain conditions both may be correct; so much depends on the nature of the soil.

In general, somewhere between these two extremes is the best plan to follow. The arduous task of trenching three feet deep is rarely necessary or advisable, and the labour entailed in wheeling soil and compost to each individual tree is scarcely less strenuous. It is usually sufficient to cultivate the top spit (about one foot) and fork over the subsoil. This can be achieved by a method known as double digging.

(21) (22)

(23) (24)

DOUBLE DIGGING

21. The soil from the first trench is placed conveniently for filling in the last trench. In this photograph the bed has been divided into two halves for easier digging of a wider bed

22. Breaking up the second spit to the full depth of the fork

23. Covering the broken-up ground of the second spit with manure

24. Forking manure into second spit in light soils

48

A trench two feet wide and one spit deep is taken out across the width of the bed. This soil with the loose crumbs from the bottom of the trench is wheeled to the far end of the bed. It is a good practice to heap this soil on a piece of hessian canvas so that it may be filled into the last trench without leaving soil on the grass path. Having dug out the first trench the subsoil is forked over but left at the bottom. If the soil is heavy, decayed leaves, coarse sand, or even cinders may be forked in so as to improve the drainage and aerate the subsoil. Some authorities advocate mixing farmyard manure in this subsoil, and this is an advantage in light soils, but in heavy soils it is wellnigh impossible to do this and its beneficial effect is doubtful. If the bed is cut out of a grass tennis court or lawn it is useful to break up the turf which has been skimmed off before trenching and place it grass side downwards on top of the subsoil. About one-half the depth of the next two-foot-wide trench is now dug into the first trench which has just been prepared, and this six-inch layer of soil mixed with well-rotted farmyard manure, or compost enriched with bone meal, hoof and horn, or other organic manure (about a quarter of a pound to each five feet run of trench). The next six inches are now transferred to the top of this. It is unwise to mix any manure in the top six inches.

When digging out the trenches it is better to work backwards at right angles to the length of the bed, as by this means the exact width of two feet of soil can be transferred to the empty trench. It also makes for clean working and enables one to keep a level surface throughout the bed. The trenches are taken out in this way until the end of the bed is reached, and then the soil from the first trench is used to fill the last empty trench.

If the soil is heavy, with a somewhat high clay content it is advisable to raise the beds some six inches above the surrounding paths. This can be done either by incorporating new soil or lowering the paths, if these are not grassed, and spreading the soil thus obtained over the beds. The raising of the beds is not necessary in light and well-drained soils, but it is a great improvement on soils which tend to become waterlogged.

The preparation of the rose beds is best done in the late summer or early autumn. If for any reason the operation cannot be carried out until late autumn it is advisable to delay planting until the spring. It is essential that newly made beds are allowed a month or two at least to settle, as it is courting failure to plant trees in soil that is full of air pockets. A few weeks of rain will settle the soil in the beds far better than any artificial methods.

One type of soil that most roses will not tolerate is that with a high chalk content. If the surface soil is very shallow on the top of the chalk rock it is advisable to purchase loads of top-spit and build up the beds. This is easier, and in the end cheaper, than laboriously digging out the chalk and filling in with new soil to a depth of twelve inches. It requires a keen rosarian to make a success of rose growing in chalk areas, though it has been done and can be done quite successfully with many of the species and shrub roses, but most gardeners will prefer to transfer their affections to plants which grow well in this type of soil.

Although the preparation of the rose beds just described sounds somewhat laborious it must be remembered that these beds will last quite a long time before they need renewal. Good roses have been grown for as many as twenty years in beds which have been properly prepared in the first instance and then given the correct surface treatment in subsequent years.

CHAPTER 4

BUYING AND PLANTING ROSE TREES

BEFORE considering planting the rose beds it is necessary to make a careful selection of the trees you wish to grow. A word of warning is necessary here: it is not altogether wise to make your selection either from a nurseryman's rose catalogue or from roses you see exhibited at shows. The former is produced, primarily, to sell the roses listed irrespective of whether or not they will suit your soil or climate; while the latter are usually grown by specialists and the blooms exhibited give little or no indication of the vigour of the trees. They may have been grown on trees limited to one, two, or three stems only, and might prove quite disappointing if planted as garden roses.

The National Rose Society publishes each year lists of roses suitable for various purposes. These lists are compiled from the votes received from a large number of knowledgeable amateur growers and of representatives of the trade. They indicate roses which grow well in the north of England and those which are more suited to the south of the country, also those best suited for hedges and those which will flourish in towns. The roses described in Chapter 12 are those of which the author has personal knowledge and are strong growers under widely differing conditions. The faults as well as the virtues of these roses are mentioned, and the would-be grower will be well advised to refer to both these sources of information before buying.

It is also helpful to visit a local nursery and the gardens of any rose enthusiasts and see for yourself how these rose trees grow under conditions similar to your own.

The order for trees should be placed with a nursery-man of repute as early as possible after June. If you wait until late in the season you may well find that the varieties you require are sold out. Orders are usually dealt with in strict rotation and are executed as soon as possible in November.

When your bundle of trees arrives, open it carefully, examine the trees and if, as sometimes happens, they have been sent out with foliage and even flower buds on the stems, cut off the leaves, leaving a little of the leaf stalk attached and shorten the stems to below any flower buds. Any damaged roots should be cut off above the bruise, and very long roots should be shortened a little. It is good practice to immerse the trees completely in a tank containing a little potassium permanganate (about one ounce in four gallons of water) or diluted Condy's Fluid, as this disinfects the trees. If your ground is not ready for planting open up a trench about a foot deep in some spare land in the garden, place the trees separately in the trench, and cover the roots and part of the stems with soil so that no harm will be caused by frost. During periods of hard frost it is well to cover the trees with straw or old sacks to provide further protection.

Planting may be done any time between November and March if the weather permits and the soil is in a reasonably dry condition. As such conditions often only occur for short periods it is well to have everything in readiness so that the most can be made of the limited time. Prepare several barrow-loads of soil mixed with about one-quarter of its bulk of peat and, if your ground is heavy, about the same bulk of sharp sand. To each barrow-load of soil add two pounds of bone meal and mix well. Keep this soil mixture dry, either by storing it under a shed or covering it with sheets of corrugated iron or a tarpaulin. The soil should be thoroughly mixed by turning it over a few times during the period of storage. See that all the tools you will require are to hand: spade, digging fork, hand trowel, rod and line, well-sharpened secateurs, and labels. A marking stick eighteen inches long will be found useful for the correct spacing of the trees, and a forked stick will help when planting the trees. When the 'good-day-for-planting' arrives take all the tools down to the site: there is nothing so time-wasting as having to make several journeys to and from the tool-shed. A barrow-load of the prepared soil should be wheeled to a convenient place near the rose bed to be planted and a bucket is useful to carry the soil along the bed as required.

Various ways of planting rose trees have been suggested from time to time. Some authorities suggest digging a circular hole and planting the tree on a slight mound of earth placed in the centre of the hole, spreading out the roots symmetrically round this mound. The trouble is that, unfortunately, when the trees arrive from the nursery, the roots are usually all growing in one direction, and it is practically impossible to make them take up a circular position. There is much to be said for planting the tree as it has been growing in the nursery, and for this purpose it will be found helpful to adopt the following method.

Dig a hole in the way illustrated (Plate 25) and of dimensions given in Figure 5. The planting operations are shown in the Plates 25–31.

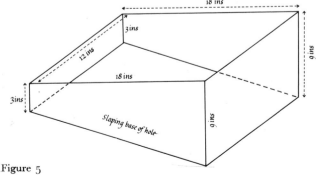

Figure 5

25. Digging the hole to receive the roots. Note the sloping floor

26. The tree is root pruned prior to planting. The stronger roots are shortened and any damaged ones are cut out

27. If the tree is being planted in March it is well to prune before planting. Trees planted in autumn must not be pruned until the following March. The illustration shows a three-year-old tree being pruned before replanting. Note that the older wood is being cut out down to the base

28. The newer wood is shortened. For further details of pruning see Chapter 5

29. The tree is held firmly near the shallow end of the hole and the roots spread out along the sloping bed, the junction of the tree and the stock being just about ground-level. Two handfuls of the prepared soil should be sprinkled over the bottom of the hole before planting, and a similar quantity worked round the roots to avoid air-pockets in the immediate neighbourhood of the roots

30. The hole filled in, either using the soil dug out if a single tree is being planted, or the soil taken from the next hole eighteen inches distant (indicated by the measuring stick). The soil is firmed by treading. If the land is heavy the treading should not be too severe, but on light soils it must be done very thoroughly. This photograph shows a tree pruned suitably for garden purposes

31. The same tree as in Plate 30 pruned 'hard', showing the depth to which the tree should be planted

32. A bed of maiden trees planted in the autumn

33. The same bed showing spring pruning

If a new bed is to be planted, e.g. one of the long rectangular beds shown in the designs of rose gardens in Chapter 2, it is important to devise a plan of operation which will obviate unnecessary movement of soil, and thus ease the labour if one is carrying out the operation single-handed. The author has found the following method (Figure 6) admirable both for labour saving and for a minimum of trampling on the bed during planting.

Divide the bed lengthwise into two equal parts by putting the line across at XY. The hole A is dug to the shape shown in Figure 5, and the shallow end eighteen inches from the shorter side of the bed. The soil from A is placed at A_1 and the tree planted in A as described above, the stem of the stock on which the tree is budded being placed in the back left-hand corner of the hole, and the roots running down the bed of the hole from the shallower to the deeper end. The tree may be held in position by a forked stick the prongs of which are pushed firmly in the ground one on each side of the stock. The soil for filling in is taken from B, which is dug in the position shown in Figure 6, and the soil firmed round the tree. The hole B is now ready to receive the second tree, which is again planted with the stem of the stock in the back left-hand corner and the soil for filling is taken from C. Then the hole D is dug and the soil used for C. This process continues until the hole P is dug and the soil

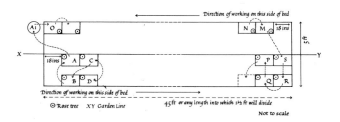

Figure 6. Suggested method for planting a long rectangular bed

from Q used to fill it after planting. Now a change is necessary; the hole R is next dug and the soil from it is used to fill Q. When R is planted the soil from S is used to fill it. The final row of trees is next planted, working from the far end of the bed in the direction shown. M is dug with the shallow end eighteen inches from the end of the bed, and the soil used for filling S. Again the tree is planted with the stem in the back left-hand corner of the hole as you face the bed, for you are now working on the other side. There is no change in the rhythm of your digging and soil moving, it still goes from right to left. The tree in M is firmed in by the soil from N. This work proceeds until the hole O is finally planted and the soil at A_1 used for filling in.

CHAPTER 5

PRUNING

MUCH has been said and written on the pruning of rose trees, so much, in fact, that the beginner is somewhat befogged. There are those who believe in hard pruning and those who advocate long pruning. Some argue that the trees should be pruned in the late autumn or early winter, while others hold tenaciously to pruning in late March or April.

Why prune at all, and what is the object of pruning? A study of the wild rose in its native habitat will provide an answer. If one studies the wild rose growing in the hedgerow it will be observed that the tree gradually becomes weak at the top, and this part of the stem finally dies. On further examination one finds a new shoot is sent out lower down on the stem. Cultivated roses left un-pruned will flower well for the first, second, and possibly the third year, but then they become weak at the top. Strong shoots are sent out lower down on the branch, and these soon take the main proportion of the sap. The older part of the branch becomes starved and ultimately dies. Nature thus provides its own method of pruning, but in our gardens it would be a very untidy and a rather slow method to apply.

A rose tree is a shrub and if left to itself would become unshapely and certainly not give of its best if never pruned. Pruning need not be a difficult task even for the beginner if the following guiding principles are observed.

First, air and light must be allowed to get into the centre of the tree; secondly, weak and diseased and very old stems must be cut away at the base or in the case of the very old stems to the lowest shoot of newer wood

34. A rose shoot showing 'eyes'. The 'eyes' indicated by arrows are new leaf buds which will later give flowering stems, and which grow at the junction of the leaf with the stem. Those which are nearer the top of the stem (indicated by arrows) are quite obvious, while those near the base can scarcely be seen, but they can be felt as slight swellings when the finger is rubbed along the stem

growing on these stems; thirdly, the strong healthy stems remaining must be shortened to a suitable outward growing eye about six or eight inches from the base.

What is an 'eye' the beginner asks, and how does one find it? A glance at the photograph (Plate 34) will make it clear.

Hard pruning means cutting the stem down to the second or third eye from the base of the shoot and should be reserved for maiden trees (i.e. trees such as you receive

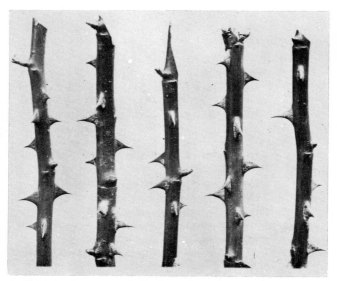

35. Right and wrong methods of pruning
    A. Cut made too high above eye
    B. Cut made too close to eye
    C. Cut badly made: too long
    D. Jagged cut showing damaged eye
    E. Cut correctly made

from the nurseryman and which were budded in the July of the previous year), or for the production of large exhibition blooms. Long or light pruning means taking off little more than the top few inches of the stem which flowered the previous season. This method tends to develop tall trees with many bare stems at the base, and only occasionally will one get strong shoots growing from the base of such stems. I have seen trees which have been pruned in this manner for several years and which have reached a height of seven or eight feet, the first two or three feet of which have been bare, thick, unsightly stems. The blooms on such trees, though sometimes fairly plentiful, are of poor quality and give little reward for labour expended in cultivating the trees.

(36)

(37)

(38)

36. Established standard tree of 'Phyllis Gold' as it appeared at the end of the flowering season

37. The same tree pruned in the following March

38. The same tree in flower in July

For ordinary garden purposes there is no doubt that moderate pruning, i.e. somewhere between these two extremes, gives the best results when once the tree is established. It certainly pays to prune fairly hard the first year after planting, except on very light soils when it is better to prune moderately the first year and hard the second year when the tree is established.

The photographs (Plates 28, 30–33) in Chapter 4 show how a three-year-old tree and also a bed of maiden trees should be pruned. Plates 36–43 show how Standards and Floribundas should be pruned.

39. Three-year-old tree of the Floribunda 'Märchenland' as it appeared at the end of the flowering season

40. Weak and old stems, particularly those growing into the middle of the tree, are removed

41. The remaining stems in process of being shortened to a suitable eye – note that shoots growing from a strong stem are shortened more than the new stems bearing no side shoots

42. The pruning completed in March

43. The same tree full of bloom the following July

Treatment of Rambler Roses

True Ramblers such as 'Dorothy Perkins', 'Excelsa', 'Albertine', 'Alberic Barbier', 'Minnehaha', 'Lady 'Godiva', 'Crimson Shower', 'Crimson Conquest', 'Easlea's Golden Rambler' generally provide long new shoots from the base each year. It is a wise practice to tie these to canes so that they do not get twisted or broken by that occasional gale one experiences during the flowering season. During September, when the flowering period is completely over, cut out all the growths which have flowered and tie in the new ones. Sometimes one finds a strong new shoot growing out of a flowering stem some distance along the stem. In this case cut the flowering stem just above the junction with the new stem and tie the latter to the support. If, as happens in some seasons,

c

(44)   (45)

44. Rambler rose 'Dr W. van Fleet', after pruning, showing laterals shortened and stems tied in to poles
45. The same trees in bloom in July

no new long stems grow from the base, retain the best of the old growths and cut back the laterals of these, which have already flowered, to two or three inches. This lack of long new stems is often characteristic of the varieties 'Dr W. van Fleet', 'Paul's Scarlet Climber', 'Chaplin's Pink', and 'American Pillar', and they will almost invariably have to be treated as described above.

A pleasing way of growing the Ramblers 'Mary Wallace', 'Chaplin's Pink', 'Sander's White' is shown in Plates 48, 49, and 50.

The method of shortening laterals is illustrated with the Rambler 'Dr W. van Fleet', grown as a pillar rose (Plates 44, 45). When three such trees are trained on the legs of a tripod they present a feature of indescribable beauty when in full bloom.

A Rambler which throws good long new shoots from the base is illustrated in the photographs of 'Crimson Shower' (Plates 46, 47).

(46)   (47)

46. Rambler rose 'Crimson Shower' after cutting out stems which have flowered and showing how the new shoots are tied to the poles

47. The same in flower in mid-August

Climbers (large flowering) and Climbing Sports

Beautiful as are the Ramblers with their great covering capacity and their large clusters of bloom, the individual blooms are of a somewhat poor quality and their attractiveness depends on the massed effect of brilliant colour. There are now many climbing roses which, in addition to producing masses of bloom, bear roses of the charm and form of the Hybrid Tea bush roses – many are in fact climbing sports of the Hybrid Teas. They can be used effectively on walls or to cover the side of a shed. The Bourbon Climber 'Zéphirine Drouhin' is shown in Plates 51 and 52 used for the latter purpose.

Two other old favourites, in their climbing form, 'Mme Caroline Testout' and 'Mme Abel Chatenay', make charming subjects when trained against a wall. Many other Hybrid Teas are now available as Climbers: 'Cl. Étoile de Hollande', 'Cl. Golden Dawn', 'Cl. Mrs

67

(48)

(49)

(50)

48. Three trees of the rambler rose 'Mary Wallace' trained on a tripod

49. Rambler rose 'Chaplin's Pink Climber' trained on an arch

50. Rambler rose 'Sander's White' trained up a post

51. Bourbon Climber 'Zéphirine Drouhin' pruned and tied to wires stretched along the side of a shed with the Floribunda 'Goldilocks' in the foreground. Note the way the laterals are shortened

52. The same in flower in July

Sam McGredy', 'Cl. Crimson Glory', 'Cl. Ena Hark-ness', are all vigorous and produce masses of large well-formed flowers in June and July, and also produce a reasonable number of blooms in the autumn. This latter feature gives them an advantage over that wonderful Climber 'Paul's Lemon Pillar' which produces very large well-formed pale lemon-yellow blooms but which is summer flowering only. The photograph (Plate 53) shows Climbing 'Golden Dawn' trained as a pillar rose.

The flowers on climbers trained in this manner always seem to grow best near the top, and if this method is used the tripods should be placed so that dwarf Hybrid Teas or Floribundas can be grown in front. I find Climbers are more pleasing if grown attached to long low supports so that the long stems can be stretched almost horizontally. Laterals then break from almost every part of the stem and the whole screen is covered with bloom. Also it must be remembered that exposure to frost and strong, cold, easterly winds will do much damage to these climbing sports, and the protection of a wall or wooden fence is desirable, if the best results are to be obtained in gardens exposed to wind and severe frost.

This account of climbing roses would be incomplete without mention of the new type of climber recently introduced by that most distinguished German hybrid-ist Kordes. They are the result of patient work on hybrid *Rugosas* and other rose species, and a number are doing well in the National Rose Society's trial ground at Oaklands, St Albans. They are hardy, continuous-bloom-ing climbers and make excellent subjects trained up single poles (Plate 54). See also p. 176.

Pruning may be done by a knife or by secateurs. In either case the instrument used must be sharp. I always use secateurs of a good quality and sharpen the blade frequently. A small tapering saw is useful for cutting thick old stems which are too hard and big for the secateurs. As in most practical processes, there is a right and a wrong way to make the cuts. If the instrument

53. Three trees of Climber 'Golden Dawn' trained on a tripod

54. New type of Climber introduced by Kordes, in bloom in the National Rose Society's trial ground in July

used is blunt the stem is inevitably crushed and the cells behind the leaf bud are damaged and cease to function. The cut should be made in the right direction, neither too high above the bud nor too low. The type of cuts to avoid and the correct type are shown in Plate 35. The above method of pruning applies to all the types of rose trees previously mentioned; if, however, you have a rose hedge which has been carefully pruned until it is well established you can then prune it as you do a privet hedge, with shears, and you will have a plethora of blossom during the summer. There is no need to prune each individual plant. Shorten some of the strong young growths in July to about one-third their length. In the following season these will be thickly set with flowering laterals.

What is the best time to prune? The short answer is any time after leaf fall, but you may find if you prune early in the winter, i.e. late December or early January, you may have to prune again when the frosts have done their damage to the young shoots. A safe guide to the inexperienced is to prune *as soon as* new growth appears. This will vary with the season and with the district in which the rose trees grow. In the south and south-west of England Floribundas may be pruned in February, Hybrid Teas and Climbers in mid-March, and Ramblers in September. In the north of England pruning may be carried out a month later. Pruning should not be carried out during frosty weather or when the tree has burst into growth. In the former case, shoots are certain to be damaged and a cut lower down will have to be made later, in the latter case sap is rising rapidly and new shoots will be weakened by the loss of sap from the pruning cut.

Much time can be saved by removing weak or dead stems immediately after the autumn flowering, and the long stems may be shortened a little to avoid the disturbing effect of winter gales.

CHAPTER 6

CULTURAL OPERATIONS

Feeding

W HAT does a rose tree require in the way of food, and how does it obtain it? It is capable, as is every tree, of building up much of its food supply by a process called photosynthesis; that is, the building up of substances by using light. This process is carried out by the leaves and is simply the indirect use of the energy of the sun to join together two common chemical compounds, carbon dioxide and water, thus forming carbohydrates (sugars, starches, cellulose) and at the same time liberating oxygen. The carbon dioxide is taken in from the air through the leaves, and the water is largely absorbed from the soil by the root hairs, though some is absorbed through the leaves.

In sunlight a rose tree builds up in its leaves a green substance called chlorophyll, and without this the above synthesis cannot take place. Chlorophyll is a complex substance and contains a number of chemical elements among which are carbon, hydrogen, oxygen, magnesium, and traces of calcium. Iron (and probably manganese) plays an important part in the formation of chlorophyll, although not actually entering into its composition. In soils which are deficient in iron salts or in which the iron salts are 'locked up' by excess of chalk, the rose trees suffer from a disease known as lime chlorosis, which causes the leaves to lose their rich green colour and become yellow. This means that the leaves will be unable to synthesize the carbohydrates necessary for the building up of the woody tissue and for storage for the subsequent liberation of energy. A manganese deficiency in the soil also produces chlorosis and causes paling of the leaves between the veins.

There are other elements which are necessary for the production of a healthy rose tree. Protoplasm, the living substance of all plants, contains nitrogen, and the rose tree must absorb this nitrogen in the form of nitrates. These are soluble in water and are taken in by the roots or may be absorbed by the leaves if sprayed on them in extremely dilute solution. Phosphates and potash are also essential for the healthy growth of the trees.

Rose trees, like other plants and animals, also breathe. They take in oxygen largely through their roots and leaves. In the process of respiration the oxygen is used to 'burn' some of the stored carbohydrates and liberate energy for the growth of the tree. During this process carbon dioxide and water vapour are given out. It is therefore just the reverse of photosynthesis. The process of respiration goes on day and night, but that of photosynthesis can only proceed in the presence of light.

The mineral salts (nitrates, phosphates, and potash) normally enter the rose tree via the roots. The roots have no chlorophyll and therefore depend on the leaves to manufacture the carbohydrate of which they are largely composed. To grow a healthy tree therefore it is essential to have healthy green foliage and a good root system. Nitrates help to form good, rich, green foliage; phosphates assist root action, and potash helps to build up a sturdy tree and give better blooms. These are the three main mineral foods, but it has been shown that traces of iron, magnesium, manganese, and boron have a part to play as well.

Although the rose beds may have been carefully prepared as described in Chapter 3, the rose trees will require some attention in the way of feeding even during the first year as well as in subsequent years. If possible, immediately after pruning, spread farmyard manure about two inches thick over the whole of the bed. If manure is not procurable a mulch of well-rotted compost,

(55)   (56)

55. Spreading fertilizer round trees before applying mulch
56. Applying mulch after hoeing in the fertilizer

leaf-mould, and peat, or spent hops, or even chopped straw should be used instead (Plate 56). If the mulch is not farmyard manure, reinforce it by sprinkling one of the proprietary rose fertilizers over the surface of the soil prior to applying the mulch (Plate 55). It is better to use one-half the amount suggested on the container and give the second half about two to three weeks later. If you wish to mix your own fertilizer the following is a most satisfactory mixture: two parts by weight of potassium nitrate (nitrate of potash), one part by weight ammonium sulphate (sulphate of ammonia), five parts by weight calcium superphosphate (superphosphate of lime), and two parts by weight of potassium sulphate. This should be sprinkled evenly over the bed, using two ounces per square yard for each of the two applications suggested (a normal handful is about four ounces). Some rose growers advocate sprinkling the fertilizer in a band round the tree about nine inches from the main stem as they believe that when the fertilizer is broadcast over the whole bed, weeds are stimulated more than in the banded method. Also it is suggested the phosphate may become chemically fixed in the soil and therefore not available to the plant,

75

whereas by concentrating it in a narrow band more remains available in solution for the plant to absorb. I have tried both methods and find little or no difference, but I live in a district where weeds grow to perfection without any encouragement!

Whichever method is used the fertilizer should be hoed lightly into the surface soil. Care should be exercised when using chemical fertilizers, and it must be remembered that a little applied at intervals of two or three weeks is far better than a large application given only once. The second and subsequent applications will, of course, be sprinkled over the surface of the mulch and need not be hoed in. If the weather continues dry for a week, overhead watering should be applied, i.e. if natural rain does not fall, apply 'artificial' rain. There is much to be said for overhead irrigation, the cold water from the hose is slightly warmed as it passes in a fine spray through the air, also it dissolves some oxygen from the air, and this is carried to the roots of the tree.

As the season progresses lawn mowings may be spread over the surface of the beds, thus renewing the mulch first applied. This mulching with organic matter is extremely important. It is probably the most important single consideration in keeping the soil in a highly fertile state. It increases the water-holding capacity, it is a storehouse for plant food, and also supplies food for the soil bacteria. In addition it gives the soil a good tilth. It also controls weeds and to some extent lessens the attacks of spore diseases which affect the leaves of the rose trees.

Most garden soils, particularly those that have grown crops for some time, become deficient in humus and inorganic fertilizers cannot make good this deficiency.

Another important factor which is often mentioned nowadays in speaking of a soil is the pH value. What does the pH value of a soil mean? Quite simply it is a scale of values (1–14) to cover the complete range of acidity and alkalinity. Soils vary very much in respect of acidity and alkalinity in various parts of the country. In Cornwall, for example, much of the soil is acid, whereas in Kent, parts of Sussex, and the Cotswolds, where the subsoil is chalk, the soil is alkaline. Soils with a pH 1–7 are acid, and the *lower* the pH number the *more acid* is the soil; soils which have a pH 7–14 are alkaline, and the alkalinity *increases with* the pH number.

Plant growth is, generally speaking, only possible between the range pH 4 to pH 8: those soils which are below pH 4 being too acid and those above pH 8 too alkaline to stimulate plant growth.

The ideal range for rose trees is 5·6 to 6·5; that is, slightly acid. Roses can be grown on soils as acid as 5·0 and as alkaline as 7·4, but more care will be required in feeding if satisfactory results are to be obtained. If the soil is more acid than 5·4 or more alkaline than 7·4 nitrification is very slow and the phosphates become relatively fixed and not available to the plant. As the soil approaches pH ranges below 5·0 compounds of calcium, magnesium, and potassium are lost by being washed out of the root zone. Also some of the more valuable trace elements like manganese and iron are relatively insoluble at low pH ranges and are therefore not readily available to the growing tree. There are soil-testing outfits on the market by which you may yourself test the pH value of your particular soil, or you can usually get this done for you by the County Horticultural Adviser.

Powdered chalk will act as a corrective of a too acid soil, and powdered green (horticultural) sulphur may be applied to reduce the alkalinity. The pH number will give you no definite indication of the *amount* of chalk or sulphur to apply, and it is best to start with small quantities and add more from time to time until the soil test gives the correct pH range. Wood ashes have a pH value about 9·0 and will therefore tend to increase the alkalinity, being for that reason very useful for acid soils. Ammonium sulphate has a pH 3·8 and its application will tend to increase acidity; it is therefore good for alkaline soils. Bone meal has a pH 5·4 and is ideal to use

77

if your soil is already within the range suitable for rose trees, but which will have little effect on the pH value of alkaline soils and no effect on the pH of acid soils. Bone meal contains no nitrogen and no potassium; it is calcium phosphate and therefore must not be regarded as a *complete* fertilizer.

All this may sound a little alarming to the would-be rose grower, but rigorous treatment will only be necessary in the relatively small areas where extremes of pH occur. Generally speaking, the soils in England are often of a suitable range without further treatment, but it is well to have your soil tested to be quite certain.

After the first flowering of the rose trees it is good practice to give a further dressing of fertilizer, and if inorganic fertilizers were used in the first instance change the diet to organic manures such as fish manure, hoof and horn, dried blood, and guano. Whichever is used, remember to use the fertilizer sparingly.

No plant food should be given after August as this will probably result in sappy growth which is certain to be affected when the frosts set in. Lawn mowings may be added as these will rot and provide more humus in the surface soil.

FOLIAR FEEDING. It used to be thought that only gases entered through the stomata of the leaf, but recent experiments both in this country and in America have shown that soluble salts may be introduced through the leaves, and foliar feeding has become quite popular in America. The solutions must be extremely dilute and may be applied in June when the foliage is mature and again after the first flowering. A mixture of urea, dihydrogen ammonium phosphate, and potassium nitrate in the proportions of $3 : 2 : 1\frac{1}{2}$ parts by weight respectively may be sprayed on the foliage in a solution containing half an ounce of the mixture per gallon of water. The spraying should be carried out on a dull, dry day and the leaves sprayed on the under side as well as the upper side.

Foliar feeding has been tried out successfully on a variety of crops with very good results, and there is no reason why its application to roses should not become more widespread with beneficial results.

Hoeing

Throughout the growing season hoeing is a most important cultural operation; not only does it remove weeds but it helps in producing a fine texture and in keeping the soil sufficiently 'open' to supply air spaces for the supply of oxygen to the roots. Hoeing as a means of conserving moisture in the soil is open to some doubt. A good mulch spread over the surface is more effective.

Treatment of Chlorosis: Chelates and Sequestrenes

The interveinal yellowing of the leaf is due to iron or manganese deficiency, possibly both. These two elements are probably involved in the formation of the protein part of the chlorophyll molecule, and any deficiency of either will offset the green colouring of the leaf. There may be much iron in your soil, but it may be rendered unavailable to plants. A high pH, overabundance of lime or chalk or phosphates ties up iron as insoluble hydroxide or carbonate or phosphate, and thus, though present, the iron is not available as plant food. Chelates and sequestrenes for the prevention and treatment of chlorosis can now be bought. These chelates are complex organic acids which contain iron in a 'bound' condition. This iron does not form insoluble salts in the soil and is available to the plant. A completely soluble chelate is sequestrene which contains twelve per cent iron. Sequestrene Plus contains both iron and manganese. One ounce in twenty-five gallons of water applied to 100 square feet of surface may be used as a preventative if applied two or three times during the growing season. If there is definite chlorosis shown in the leaves one level teaspoonful per plant thoroughly watered in will effect a cure.

79

57. *Iron deficiency.* Showing the gradation in chlorosis. Left: youngest leaf which is entirely chlorotic. Centre and Right: less chlorotic leaves, showing green vein pattern

58. *Manganese deficiency.* Showing the development of the typical interveinal chlorosis (or paling). Compare with iron deficiency pattern

For use on both acid and alkaline soils, Sequestrene 330 is effective.

Chlorosis and other deficiency diseases which affect the leaves are illustrated in Plates 57–61. These may be controlled by the correct dressing of the beds with organic manures and suitable proprietary fertilizers.

59. *Nitrogen deficiency*. Note small size of leaves. They are pale green with yellow and red tints. The spots shown are red and always accompany the deficiency

60. *Magnesium deficiency*. The centres of the leaves become pale and areas of dead tissue develop near the mid-rib

61. *Potassium deficiency*. Brown patches develop around the leaf margins, which eventually form a continuous brown rim of dead tissue (marginal leaf scorch). Brown areas may also develop between the veins

CHAPTER 7

DISEASES AND PESTS AND HOW TO DEAL WITH THEM

Rose trees in common with other forms of life are subject to pests and diseases. Fortunately for the rose grower there are means of dealing with them. The healthier the tree, the less liable it is to attack, and so the first consideration is good cultivation. Bad drainage, over-feeding, or using an ill-balanced fertilizer, are among the greatest causes of ill health in the tree, so see to it that these things are attended to with the utmost care. Even when all the care possible has been given there are climatic conditions to contend with, and these are beyond human control. A warm humid climate is more suited to the spread of disease than a cool dry one. Also, certain diseases like Black Spot and Rust are very rarely seen in industrial areas. Whether or not these areas will be immune when smoke and sulphur fumes are eliminated from the air is at present a matter of conjecture; we have not yet reached that stage in industrial development. I do not propose to deal with a long list of pests and diseases, which in itself would be depressing and almost enough to deter anyone from growing roses. In any case many of the troubles one might list may never occur, so why worry?

Three diseases which must be mentioned are Mildew, Black Spot, and Rust.

MILDEW (*Sphaerotheca pannosa*) (Plate 62) is easily recognized and is probably the commonest fungal disease of the rose and one which, unless checked, can be most destructive. The whitish spots which first appear on the

83

young leaves soon spread and cover the leaf with a white powder. It often attacks young buds, and the outer layer may decay before the bud can open and the flower is ruined. Contrary to the common idea, damp weather is not the cause of mildew. Rose mildew must not be confused with the green mould which often appears on organic matter during damp weather. Hot days followed by cold nights, with the general accompaniment of heavy dew (which provides sufficient water for spore germination), are the conditions which cause rose mildew. The enclosed garden, which is conducive to stagnant air, is usually subject to mildew attacks.

Buisol white oil emulsion, which is colloidal cuprous oxychloride mixed with a white oil, is an effective deterrent. Karathane is also most effective and will quickly check a severe attack. These proprietary substances are easily obtainable and care should be taken to follow the directions as to the suitable strength to be used. If too strong, damage to foliage is almost certain to occur. Also it is well to remember that any mixture containing copper compounds must not be diluted in galvanized vessels; wooden or enamel or polythene buckets must be used.

Rose trees should be sprayed early in the season, the first application being given immediately after pruning. The stems and the surface soil should be thoroughly drenched and the finer the spray the more effective it will be. There are many good spraying apparatuses on the market ranging from the ordinary garden syringe to an elaborate electrically controlled apparatus. For a small garden a hand syringe which gives a fine spray is quite sufficient. The knapsack type of apparatus is usually made of brass or some other alloy which does not react with any of the copper compounds present in certain preparations used for spraying. One straps a three-gallon container over the shoulders and it has a long hand-sprayer attached, which is useful when several hundred trees have to be treated and when the user has sufficient

62. Rose Mildew

strength to carry the thirty pounds about the garden!
For my part I prefer the pump type in which about a
quart of the spray to be used is submitted to pressure by
pumping air into the container. On releasing the pressure
by a hand-controlled lever a fine spray is ejected. These
sprayers are easy to carry about and are economical in
use, as the spray is delivered in a very fine mist which has
a great covering capacity. When the tree is in full leaf
the leaves should be sprayed on both sides and the stems
also should be thoroughly wetted. The best time to spray
is in the evening when the sun is low. If spraying is done
in the sunshine, leaf scorch is almost inevitable, and the
tree may be suspected of having some other disease!

BLACK SPOT (*Diplocarpon rosae*). In districts where attacks of black spot (Plate 63) are liable to occur, such as the south and south-west of England and South Wales, it is well to take time by the forelock and spray in anticipation of an attack. Sprays such as we have at present are preventative in their action. It is too late to spray when once an attack has started, as it spreads so rapidly. In my garden in the south-west I have seen trees apparently quite free from the disease one day and within a matter of three or four days the whole garden has been riddled with black spot. A wet warm climate is conducive to the rapid spread of the disease, and it is quite common (unless protective measures are taken) to see a rose garden in the south-west completely defoliated by the end of August. The disease is easily recognized by the appearance on the leaves of black spots with fringed edges.

My experience is that the lower leaves are first attacked, but so rapid is the spread of the disease that the whole tree is soon infected. Once it has been seen in the garden take precautions and spray early next season. One spraying is not sufficient but the operation should be repeated at intervals of about three weeks until the flower buds are showing colour. After the first crop of bloom it is well to spray again to prevent new growths being attacked.

Buisol white oil emulsion is an effective deterrent. Orthocide (Captan) is even better, but it must never be mixed with the *oil* emulsion. Ordinary Buisol *without the white oil* can be mixed with Orthocide without detriment. The one disadvantage of Orthocide is that it leaves a white deposit on the leaves, but this is washed off by subsequent rain.

Black spot rarely attacks rose trees before the end of June as the optimum temperature for the germination of the spores is about 70°F. A wet and warm July is ideal for the spread of the disease. Attacks are very slight in a dry season.

63. Black Spot on rose leaf

Rust (*Phragmidium mucronatum*) (Plate 64). This is to the rose tree as fatal as is lung cancer to humans, or foot and mouth disease to animals. It is a killer and needs rigorous treatment. Fortunately the climatic conditions in England are rarely suitable for a severe attack, but occasionally one occurs which is disastrous. Such an attack occurred in 1930 when the disease was widespread throughout the country. In 1956 south-west England and South Wales suffered a very severe attack, and thousands of trees were completely destroyed. The dry summer of 1955 followed by an abnormally dry spring with cold north-east winds seemed to be ideal for the spread of the disease.

64. Rose rust

In July the undersides of the leaves become covered with orange-coloured spores which later (during August) become black. The leaves are unable to perform their function of food-building and the new shoots which appear take on a reddish colour, droop, and finally shrivel. Once the disease has become well established on the trees there is nothing one can do except burn the worst affected ones, and take off and burn all the leaves from those less affected. Spraying with Buisol or with Thiram is the most effective preventative, but it must be applied *before* the attack takes place. Orthocide is not effective against rust.

Mildew, black spot, and rust can all be controlled by spraying with a mixture of Buisol (*not the white oil variety*) and Orthocide from pruning time onwards. One table-spoonful of Buisol and half an ounce of Orthocide to four gallons of water is a suitable strength to use. Deficiency diseases have already been dealt with in Chapter 6.

65. Colony of Greenfly on rose buds

Pests

The commonest pests which trouble the rose grower are
(*a*) greenfly, (*b*) the caterpillars of the rose tortrix moth,
(*c*) thrips, (*d*) the chafer beetles and their grubs. There
are others, but I propose only to deal with these four.

GREENFLY (Plates 65–6). This is so common as to
need no description, though the colour of the aphids is
not always green but may be pink or brown. They are
sucking insects and feed on the juices of young leaves and
buds. The larva of the ladybird feeds on them, and the
grey elongated grubs with a stripe of darker colour running the length of the body should on no account be
destroyed. They are the friends of the gardener and

should be encouraged as they do no harm to the trees and remove hundreds of greenfly.

Derris, Sybol, and Lindane are all effective sprays against greenfly and should be applied immediately the first greenflies are seen.

THE CATERPILLARS OF THE ROSE TORTRIX MOTH. These are of two kinds, the green and the brown. The green variety attacks the young leaves. The fatter brown variety attacks the flower bud, and a keen watch is necessary if it is to be caught before damage is done. Both varieties wrap themselves in the young leaves near the flower bud in the daytime (Figure 7) and do their destructive work by night. Hand picking is the most effective method of dealing with them. Dusting with D.D.T. is effective, but unfortunately this kills the larvae of the ladybirds and as they seem to appear about the same time (usually during May or early June) I prefer to pick the grubs by hand.

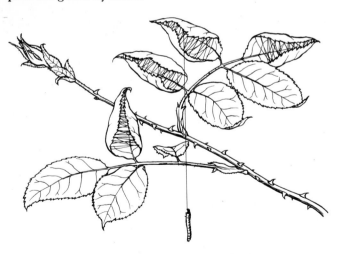

Figure 7. Caterpillar of the Rose Tortrix Moth, showing young leaves affected

66. Greenfly on rose shoot

THRIPS. These are very tiny four-winged flies about one-twentieth of an inch long which attack the flower buds just as they are opening. Roses like 'Ophelia' and 'Madame Butterfly' seem to suffer more than other varieties, but after a dry spring they seem to attack all varieties indiscriminately. The petals of the young flowers have a burnt appearance round the edges, and the flower becomes malformed (Plate 67). D.D.T. dusted on the buds just as they are opening is the best remedy.

CHAFER BEETLES AND THEIR GRUBS. There are three main species of chafers which attack roses: (*a*) the cockchafer, (*b*) the garden chafer, and (*c*) the rose chafer. They are often seen in May and June and they attack the foliage, buds, and blooms. Sometimes one sees a bloom half of which is chafed away as though it had been

67. Young flowers of roses infected with Thrips

rubbed on the thorns of a neighbouring rose stem
(Plate 68). Not only do the adult chafers cause damage
but the larvae which live in the soil feed on the roots of
the trees, causing extensive damage. The larvae of all
three varieties are very similar and are seen when one is
digging the ground. They are dirty white grubs about
one and a half inches long (Plate 69) and move very
sluggishly when out of the soil. It is best to kill as many
as possible when digging as they are difficult to eradicate
later. A dressing of Gammexane (Benzene hexachloride)
applied to the soil in early June is effective in keeping
away the egg-laying chafers. Garden and rose chafers
may be destroyed by spraying with D.D.T. emulsion to
which Pyrethrex has been added.

For further information about the life histories of the
pests described in this chapter the reader is referred to a
publication of the National Rose Society, *The Enemies of
the Rose* by John Ramsbottom and G. Fox Wilson.

68. Garden Chafer on damaged rose bud

69. Larva of Cockchafer

93

CHAPTER 8

PROPAGATION OF ROSES

Cuttings

Roses may be increased by cuttings or by budding on an established stock. Much has been said and written on the merits of propagation by cuttings rather than by budding, but I am yet to be convinced that cuttings, particularly of the Hybrid Teas, make the best and the longest-lived trees. No really conclusive experiments have been tried over a period of years to establish such merits. It is perfectly true that certain varieties root easily from cuttings, e.g. Ramblers and the Poulsen hybrid Polyanthas, and good trees may be established after a few years, but you must be prepared to wait before you get a good display of roses. If you want good and quick results it is far better to buy trees budded on a good understock by expert budders, or to bud your own stocks. It is well to know how to take cuttings in case you wish to make your own stocks for budding, such as briar cuttings or *rugosa*, or if you wish to increase your stock of Ramblers.

Take the cutting from well-ripened shoots of the current year's growth. This should be done in August or early September. The cuttings should be about a foot long and about the thickness of an ordinary pencil. Cut horizontally just below an eye and make a sloping cut just above the top eye. Cut off the lower leaves but leave some at the top. It is advisable to remove the eyes except two or three at the top which will remain above ground. Cut them out with a sharp knife, making two cuts, one above and one below, so as to remove a small wedge. This will prevent the bud developing and causing suckers to grow.

Damp the end of the cutting on wet cotton wool or

70. Rose cuttings inserted in a trench

blotting-paper, dip it in the hormone-producing powder Seradix B, and insert in a previously prepared V-shaped trench about nine inches deep containing a layer of sand one or two inches deep (Plate 70). It is best to make a hole in the sand with a cane before inserting the cutting so that it will stand upright while the soil is being packed around and finally trodden firmly. After planting, the cuttings should be watered. Put the cuttings about six inches apart and leave them until the following autumn, when they may be transplanted.

BUDDING. There is something very satisfying about budding a tree yourself, and if you have the time it is worth trying. Your nurseryman will probably spare you a few understocks. On the rich loamy soils which are fairly common in Britain the best understock is the *canina* seedling briar. On light sandy soils *multiflora* or *laxa* stocks may produce better results. It is not my purpose in this small book to discuss the merits of various understocks. This is a very big problem which can only be solved by long and carefully conducted experiments. For the beginner it will suffice to describe the *process* of budding – which is the same for any understock.

Assuming you obtain a few seedling briars in November, plant them as you would bushes but not more than a foot apart. Plant them firmly but not too deep, only just covering the inch or so of the stem between the roots and the branches. They will remain in this position until the time for budding in late July or early August. When

95

you are ready to bud remove the soil with a trowel so that the stem in which the bud is to be inserted is free from surrounding soil. Clean the short stem (about an inch) with a duster so that no soil can get into the incision when it is made. Select the wood from which the bud is to be taken from a healthy tree, using a long stem which has borne a perfect flower. Cut off all the leaves from the stem, leaving an inch of the leaf stalk to serve as a handle. Remove all thorns; if these flick off easily without tearing any bark the wood is usually ripe and suitable for providing buds. The wood must not be too young or too old. The best buds are those near the middle of the stem. Those at the top, just below the flower, are often too advanced and those near the base too recessed. These should not be used. Usually about three good buds can be obtained from a stem about a foot long. The stems should be put in water as soon as they are cut, to keep the buds fresh.

TAKING THE BUD. Hold the stem firmly in the left hand, exerting pressure with the first finger behind and slightly above the bud, and the thumb some distance below it and on the opposite side of the stem. Take the budding knife in the right hand with the face of the blade sloping downwards, the cutting edge being inclined slightly towards the middle of the stem. Cut into the bark about half an inch above the bud (Figure 8a), and, with the thumb of the right hand pressing on the stem below the bud but above the left thumb, cut behind the bud (Figure 8b). When the cutting edge is immediately behind the bud incline the blade of the knife slightly upwards towards the outside of the stem, continuing to cut until the outer skin and the right thumb is reached. A quick pull will then give you a long strip of bark which will make the next step easier. Now take the bud, complete with the part of the stem just cut out, in the left hand and with the right hand pull the long strip of bark gently (Figure 8c) so as to free the bud from the wood

96

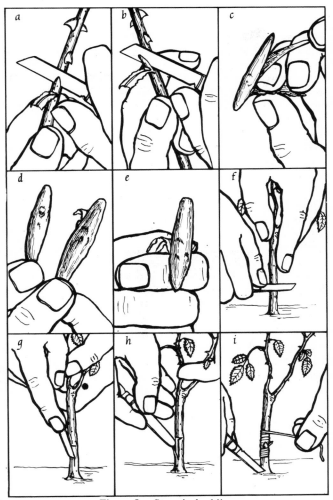

Figure 8.   Steps in budding

(Figure 8d). Trim the bark so that it is the right length to fit the available stem of the stock (sometimes this is only an inch long) (Figure 8e). Make a horizontal cut in the bark of the stock (Figure 8f) and then a vertical one, starting as near to the roots of the stock as possible and finishing at the horizontal cut (Figure 8g). Do not cut too deeply, just sufficient to be able to free the bark. Starting at the top of the cut, use the flat end of the budding knife to open the bark (Figure 8h), insert the bud and tie in with raffia (Figure 8i). Bind the raffia fairly tightly just below and above the bud and finish by slipping the end of the raffia under the last complete round. It is advisable to cut the raffia beforehand into lengths about eighteen inches long, and it should be about a quarter of an inch wide. If the raffia is dry it can be made more workable by dipping a bundle in water and then shaking it out before use.

Carefully put back the soil until it is level with the bud. After about three weeks examine the ties and if they appear to be causing a swelling below the bud ease them a little. I often cut a few strands with a sharp knife, being careful not to touch the bark. The buds and the complete growing stock will now be left to grow until the middle of February, when the head of the root stock is cut away completely just above the sheath of the bud. By this time the raffia should have rotted away; any remaining should be carefully removed. Insert a cane in the ground in a convenient place so that the growing shoot may be tied to it as soon as possible. It is some time before the junction of the new shoot and the root stock is sufficiently firm to prevent the young tree being blown out of the stock. Sometimes a bud will break quite early, even before the stock is headed back. If this happens pinch the shoot back to two eyes to get extra stems and a stronger tree. The tree which develops from the budding is called a 'maiden' tree, and it will give excellent blooms in July. It should be left to bloom *in situ*, and may be transplanted in the autumn.

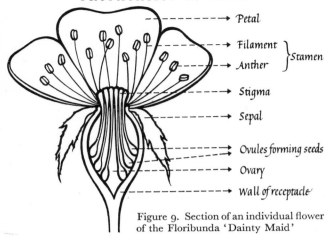

Figure 9. Section of an individual flower of the Floribunda 'Dainty Maid'

Raising New Roses. Hybridizing

Before undertaking this interesting side of rose culture it is important to understand the function of the various parts of a flower. The essential organs of the rose, as indeed of any flower, are those concerned with the production of sexual cells. They are the male and female parts of the flower. The male organ (*androecium*) consists of the stamens. A stamen consists of an anther containing pollen sacs which hold the pollen and which is situated at the top of a stalk called the filament. The female organ (*gynaecium* or pistil) comprises the carpels. The sticky top of the pistil is called the stigma. The ovary in which are found the ovules is the expanded lower part of the carpels. This is connected with the stigma by a thinner portion called the style. The non-essential organs comprise the sepals, petals, and nectaries.

A vertical section of one of the individual flowers of the Floribunda 'Dainty Maid', showing the various organs, is illustrated in Figure 9. The narrow base of each petal bears a nectary.

99

Pollination is the transference of pollen from the stamen to the stigma. This may take place in any particular rose, the pollen from the anther just dropping on the stigma. This is called self-pollination. Or the pollen may be taken from the stamens of one rose and transferred to the stigma of another. This is called cross-pollination. The process may be carried out indiscriminately by the wind or by insects which fly from flower to flower, but there is no sort of guarantee that this method will produce seeds which will give a good rose.

Hybridists go to work in a much more scientific manner. They choose each parent with care, having regard to the characteristics which they possess. The flower chosen to be the female parent first has the petals removed by a sharp knife or a long-pointed pair of scissors. This should be done before the pollen is ripe, i.e. before the rose is fully open. The stamens are then removed by cutting the filaments about a quarter of an inch above the junction with the receptacle. It is preferable to do all this under glass as it is generally difficult for the rose-hips to ripen out of doors in this country, also it is necessary to protect the reproductive parts from the weather, as well as from pollen-carrying insects.

The exposed stigma will not be ripe so it must be protected by a paper or a polythene bag for a few days. The flower chosen to be the male parent is allowed to grow naturally, and when fully open the ripe pollen grains may be seen dropping from the pollen sacs. Some of these are gathered on a camel-hair brush, or even on the finger and transferred to the sticky stigma. This sticky substance induces germination of the pollen grains, and pollen tubes are put out. The production of a pollen tube may be observed by placing a few pollen grains on a drop of sugar solution and watching them with the aid of a microscope.

The pollen tube makes its way down the conducting tissues of the style into the ovary, where a portion of the contents passes into the ovule. The ripened ovule

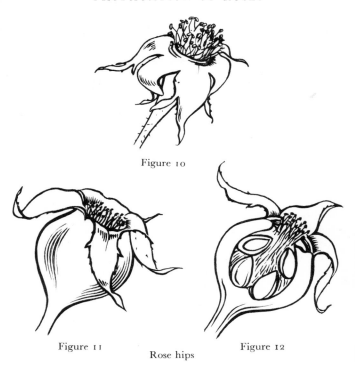

Figure 10

Figure 11

Rose hips

Figure 12

becomes the seed. Many such pollen grain tubes pass through the style and as many seeds are formed as there are ovules fertilized. The whole of the receptacle gradually ripens and produces the familiar rose-hip. The rose-hips are ripe by autumn and should be buried in wet peat in a seed-pan which is kept outside but away from mice, as these creatures have a special liking for rose seeds. When the fleshy wall of the receptacle has rotted, the seeds are extracted and put in water. Any that float are probably sterile and should not be used. Sow the rest in sterilized shallow pans or boxes in sterilized soil containing a little vermiculite. It is easier for the beginner to

Figure 13. Seed-pan showing placing of seeds

buy the sterilized John Innes Seed Compost rather than trouble to make his own mixture. Place the seeds on the surface about an inch apart and press them down a little into the soil, finally covering them with a sprinkling of the compost. Water well, using a fine-rose watering-can. Then cover with a thin layer of coarse, sharp sand, to help to prevent the formation of moss.

Some of the seeds sown in January will give seedlings in March or April, others will grow on later. When the seedlings have formed their first true leaves transplant them into a box of the same compost several inches apart and grow them on to flower. Do not expect too much! Many will be quite useless and will have to be discarded, but others which show more promise may be potted in John Innes Compost No. 1 in five-inch pots. After these have flowered select the best and bud them on small seedling stocks in the open garden. It is after this stage that the first assessment of the real worth of the seedlings can be made, but they must be budded on stocks for another year or two before you can be at all certain of a winner! Even then you will have to send half a dozen trees for a three-year trial in the National Rose Society's Trial Ground at St Albans before your new rose can be considered for an award.

From this you will gather that hybridizing requires infinite care and patience, and the hybridist who receives a Gold Medal award is to be congratulated on his achievement, but it provides an absorbing hobby for the amateur who has time to devote to it.

CHAPTER 9

GROWING ROSES UNDER GLASS

Growing roses under glass is regarded by many as an art difficult to master, expensive to achieve, and necessitating a great deal of work and worry. In fact it is nothing of the kind. Any amateur possessing even a small greenhouse which can be moderately heated for a few weeks of the year – either by electric tubular heating or by oil burners – can grow roses of the finest quality. If one is prepared to wait until early May for the blooms no heat at all is necessary beyond just sufficient to keep out the frost in the severest weather. It is the fine quality and perfection of form obtainable under glass which makes it so well worth doing. By no other means can roses be grown so free from disease, so perfect in form, and with every item of cultivation so absolutely under the control of the cultivator. Anyone who grows roses extensively in the garden knows so well the practical impossibility of achieving out of doors any measure of control over weather conditions. Everyone knows that late frost which shrivels the promising bud-bearing shoots, that gale of wind which tears the foliage, and that heavy rainstorm which usually chooses for its devastating effects the very day when one is cutting for a show or for a special display in the home. These worries never arise when cultivating under glass. Also the rose-blooming season can be prolonged to eight or nine months of the year and may even be extended to the whole twelve months by the help of a heated greenhouse and a few garden frames.

Many lovers of roses who already grow roses well in the garden would like to start a few in a small greenhouse, the question which arises is how to start and when.

There are four ways of beginning a greenhouse collection : (A) The roses may be bought in pots from certain trade growers. They are not easy to obtain and not always can one get the varieties one wants, and the method is expensive. (B) Trees may be bought from the nurseryman. These should be budded as low on the stock as possible, and if you tell him the trees are for potting up he will usually give you the kind you need. The rose trees should be potted up as soon as they arrive, so do please have your potting mixture ready in good time. (C) Your own garden trees can be dug up, root-pruned, and planted in pots in October. These pots should be stood outside until mid-December. They should be stood in a fairly sheltered position so that the autumn gales do not damage the trees or disturb them in their pots. If for any reason you cannot pot up the trees until March they should be kept out of doors until the following December. (D) Rooted *rugosa* stocks, particularly half- or quarter-standards, may be potted up in November, budded the following June, and brought into the cold greenhouse in late November or early December. This last method is the one I prefer and the one which gives me the best results.

A word of advice about the greenhouse : if you are purchasing a new one try to get one with ventilators the whole length of both sides and top. This is the ideal house but it is by no means essential. Good results can be obtained in any type of greenhouse provided there is some side and top ventilation.

Assuming the pots are brought indoors in early December, no artificial heat will be necessary until mid-January. The ventilators should be kept open, and even if there is a sharp frost it will do no harm. Towards the end of January on bright and sunny days still more ventilation may be given, and if possible it should be given from the roof. About this time the trees will break into life, and frost should be excluded by a little artificial heat. On no account must ventilators be completely closed and the temperature should not fall below 45°F.

In January and February the aim should be to keep the temperature of the house between a day maximum of 60°F. and a night minimum of 45°F. In March the corresponding temperatures should be 70°F. and 60°F. It is during April that your skill as a rose grower will be thoroughly tested. There will be occasions when the temperature runs up to 100°F. at midday, and if you are not careful with the heating it may drop to 50°F. at night. It is then that judgement, skill, and knowledge will prevail. A little shading will be necessary to prevent scorching of the leaves. I find old net curtains arranged so as to slide along picture cord very effective, and they have the merit of being cheap. The curtains can be closed on the sunny days and opened on the dull ones. Sheets of polythene tacked on the inside of the wooden window framing, thus forming double windows with an air space between the polythene and the glass, provide excellent insulation and the night temperature will be maintained a few degrees higher than it otherwise would be.

POTTING MIXTURE. Almost every grower has his own particular potting mixture, and if it produces good roses my advice is, keep to it. The following formula is one I have used for many years and found very satisfactory:

5 bushels of turfy loam chopped thoroughly and put through a half-inch sieve,
½ bushel of bonfire ashes which have been kept dry,
1 lb. bone meal,
2 lb. hoof and horn,
½ gallon of old soot.

This mixture is prepared some time before it is required and turned over several times. It is of course kept in a dry place. When potting up trees I use a ten-inch pot as I wish the tree to build up a good root system that will last for several years, also the surface of the soil is sufficiently large to permit of effective top dressing.

After covering the drainage hole with several pieces of broken porous plant-pot, put a layer, about one inch thick, of half-inch bones mixed with quarter-inch charcoal. Above this put a layer two inches thick of chopped turf (not too fine) mixed with well-matured manure. The potting mixture of the given formula is used for surrounding the roots of the tree and filling up the pot to within one to one and a half inches of the top. When planting, it is extremely important to work the soil round the roots and pack it firmly round the sides of the pot, using a wooden rod of about one inch diameter.

The rose trees should be kept dry for a fortnight after being brought into the greenhouse in December, and any remaining leaves will then drop off. Pruning is best done about Christmas and the pruning should be really hard. It is well to prune back to one or two buds of the previous year's growth; in other words, cut back every year into the old wood (Plates 71–3).

After pruning give one watering and then leave until new growth begins. Even then it must not be overdone. A really good drink once a week is sufficient at this early stage. The best time for watering is early morning, and the water should be at the same temperature as the house. About the middle of February the trees should be in very active growth and watering may be more frequent. An occasional watering, say once a week, with very weak manure water (made from cow and pig manure and soot put in a bag and submerged in a tank of water and diluted when used) will assist the trees in their growth. Towards the end of March weekly waterings with chemical manures may be given. This needs care, and I have found that a mixture of half an ounce nitrate of ammonia and half an ounce phosphate of potash dissolved in two gallons of water and given once a week during the second half of March and then twice a week when the flower buds first appear is all that is necessary for excellent blooms. Nitrogen, phosphorus, and potassium are all supplied by this formula. Foliar feeding as suggested in Chapter 6 may be used with satisfactory results.

Pests can be controlled with ease under glass. Daily spraying with clean cold water from the time the leaves appear until the buds show colour does much. If any greenfly appear introduce a little Abol Derris into the water.

Careless ventilation and rapid changes in temperature usually result in an attack of mildew. Green sulphur blown on the leaves with a small bellows controls the attack. If the greenhouse is heated with pipes, paint them, about a yard at a time if the house is about fifteen by nine feet and less for a smaller house, every fortnight with a mixture of half a pound of flowers of sulphur added to a bucketful of whitewash (made from builders' lime). The fumes are sufficient to prevent mildew and do no harm to the trees. Spraying with Karathane is also most effective.

Caterpillars, which can be troublesome under glass, must be picked off by hand. They are easily spotted by the habit they have of curling themselves in the leaves quite near the flower bud.

If large blooms are required side buds should be removed as early as possible, leaving one only which can be used if anything happens to the main bud. As soon as the main bud shows colour this final side bud can be removed if so desired.

Towards the end of April the results of one's labours become apparent in superb blooms of a quality and freshness impossible to obtain in the open garden. The roses will remain a long time on the trees as there is no wind or rain to ruin them.

After the first cut, the roses are allowed to bloom as they will and the trees are gradually cooled off preliminary to removal to the open air in June. The pots are stood in rows and all the half-standards put together, and the stems tied to a wire stretched the length of the row. To reduce the watering, which is necessary in dry

71. The rose before pruning

72. The rose after light pruning

73. The rose after hard pruning

weather, I usually sink the pots in a spare part of the kitchen garden. No further attention is necessary, beyond taking off any buds which form on new shoots, until October, when the year begins again. Each pot is examined for drainage, weeds, and worms, and the top inch or so of soil removed. A top dressing consisting of the potting mixture previously described enriched with a little bone meal (a dessertspoonful per pot) and a handful of powdered, well-matured, and dry manure. The pots are then returned to their out-of-doors position until it is time to bring them under glass again in late November or early December.

Here is a list of thirty varieties which the author has found highly satisfactory for growing as pot plants under glass. Many of them are described in detail in Chapter 12 and the predominant colour only is mentioned here.

'Barbara Richards', maize. 'Bridal Robe', creamy-white. 'Charles Mallerin', dark velvety-crimson. 'Crimson Glory', deep crimson. 'Dorothy Anderson', pink. 'Ena Harkness', scarlet-crimson. 'Ellinor le Grice', yellow. 'Ethel Sanday', yellow flushed apricot. 'Golden Dawn', pale yellow. 'Julien Potin', yellow. 'Karl Herbst', bright red. 'Lady Sylvia', pink. 'Lal', pink. 'Margaret', pale pink. 'Mary Wheatcroft', coppery flame. 'McGredy's Yellow', 'McGredy's Ivory', 'Moonbeam', yellow. 'Mrs Charles Lamplough', creamy-white. 'Mrs Sam McGredy', coppery orange. 'Ophelia', very pale pink. 'Peace', yellow edged with pink. 'Phyllis Gold', yellow. 'Picture', pink. 'Rex Anderson', creamy white. 'Show Girl', pink. 'Sir Henry Segrave', pale yellow. 'Spek's Yellow', golden yellow. 'The Doctor', 'Wm Moore', pink.

CHAPTER 10

THE SHRUB GARDEN

HERE is a delightful opportunity for the rose lover
to display some of the larger-growing Hybrid Teas, the
hybrid perpetuals, species, and their hybrids; in fact, to
mingle the old with the new. No rose garden is really
complete without at least a few of the old roses, some of
which will serve as reminders of the parentage of our
more modern types. Nor are all the shrub roses which
lay claim for a place in this part of the garden by any
means old. Some are extremely modern but their habit
of growth makes them more suitable subjects for the
shrub garden than for beds devoted to bush roses.

Many of these shrubs are seen at their best grown on
banks partially shaded by trees, but care must be taken
to see that they have a good root run and are not covered
by the branches of large forest trees. Although many of
the shrub roses will grow and produce flowers when
given little or no attention, very much better results are
obtained if the land is well prepared and manured before
they are planted, and if from time to time they are given
a top dressing containing fertilizers. Many of them grow
quite well on chalky soils.

Bulbs of all kinds, primroses, and polyanthuses can be
grown amongst them and will provide colour in the
spring before the roses appear. Little pruning is required
beyond removing dead or old wood and trimming to
keep the bush within bounds.

Those wishing to start a collection of shrub roses will
find the following list helpful. It is by no means exhaus-
tive, but it is representative and will provide a good
variety of colour.

ROSA ALBA, which is probably a hybrid of *R. damascena* and *R. canina*, is the 'White rose of Yorkshire'. Three varieties recommended are:

(i) *R. alba* 'Königin von Dänemark' (Queen of Denmark). The leaves are greyish. The flowers, which are a rich pink in the bud, pale as they open, but retain some of the pink in the centre of the bloom. They are very fragrant. The bush grows to about 6 feet in height.

(ii) *R. alba* 'Great Maiden's Blush'. A strong grower with extremely sweet fragrance. The flowers are flat and show pale pink at the centre, fading to a creamy colour at the edges.

(iii) *R. alba maxima*. This will please those who wish a purer white. It is very similar to the 'Great Maiden's Blush', but its colour is creamy-white. It grows 6 to 8 feet high.

R. BANKSIAE. China. Var. *banksiae*. Double white, a strong climber on a warm wall and in light or well-drained soil. Should be left unpruned as it flowers on the sub-laterals.

R. banksiae var. *lutea*. Double yellow, grows vigorously in the south-west of England, particularly if trained on a house wall facing south. It reaches a height of 30 feet, covering the whole wall, and is a colourful sight in summer.

BOURBON ROSES. Hybrids of *R. chinensis* and *R. damascena*. Long pruning and occasional removal of old stems is all the treatment they require. Two varieties recommended are:

(i) 'Zéphirine Drouhin', which is a thornless and semi-climbing rose admirably suited to training on a wooden fence or shed. Its flowers are cerise-pink and are very fragrant (Plate 52).

(ii) 'Mme Pierre Oger' is a most charming representative of this group. Its flowers are cream with a suggestion of pale pink. As they age they change to

74. Rose 'Mme Pierre Oger'

a rosy red. It gives a succession of flowers throughout the summer and early autumn (Plate 74).

R. CANTABRIGIENSIS. This hybrid of *R. hugonis* and *R. omeiensis* is a large single primrose yellow, much more vigorous than *R. hugonis*. Makes a showy shrub 8 to 10 feet high and of equal width.

R. CENTIFOLIA. A cross between *R. moschata* and *R. alba*. This rose is known as 'The Rose of Provence' or 'Cabbage Rose'. It is 'The rose of a hundred leaves' and was a great favourite with artists of the past. The varieties most pleasing are:

(i) 'Tour de Malakoff' makes a very large bush with good-sized blooms produced in great abundance. The buds show a lilac-pink colour and the fully opened flowers show petals with an intense violet shade.

(ii) 'Blanchefleur'. A double white rose. The tree has a vigorous habit.

(iii) 'Fantin Latour'. This is classed by some authorities as a Bourbon rose, and although not purely a Centifolia it has many of the requirements of this class. The flowers are large and flat but very beautiful. They are a delicate pink colour. Justifiably, it is an old favourite.

R. centifolia muscosa. 'The Moss Rose'. Edward Bunyard in his book on *Old Garden Roses* says of the Moss Rose: 'The Victorian age would have seemed incomplete without the Moss Rose, so firmly did it entwine the hearts of those amiable days. Valentines and scrapbooks shared its portrait and its "message" in the language of flowers. Before its day it would seem that no grace or charm could be added to the Rose. Beauty's last word had been said. But when it was found that the Rose could look cosy as well as beautiful by adding a little moss no wonder that hearts were stormed. Cosiness lay at the very centre of Victorian taste.' Not only does the moss and bristles of these roses provide cosiness, they also supply a picturesque quality.

The Common Moss Rose, which is a sport of *R. centifolia*, has rather large pink flowers. Its perfume is that of the old-time Provence type, rich and heavy. 'Nuits de Young' is a variety which should be included in any collection. There is nothing quite like

75. Another good Bourbon rose is 'Honorine de Brabant', a pale
lavender-pink rose with deeper markings

this Moss Rose with its small dark leaves and miniature double blooms, which are almost grape black.
The bush has erect stems and grows to a height of
4 to 5 feet.

R. CHINENSIS. The original species seems to have
been lost and is known only in the hybrid forms which
were cultivated by the Chinese many centuries ago.
They gave the perpetual flowering qualities to our
modern roses. The following are good varieties to
grow:

(i) 'Cecile Brunner'. This beautiful variety with
its shell-pink miniature roses of perfect shape,
reminiscent before fully open of the tiny roses on
Dresden china ornaments, should certainly be
grown. It is continuously in flower during the summer and autumn; 2 feet 6 inches high.

(ii) 'Bloomfield Abundance', a sport from 'Cecile
Brunner' which grows much taller, is shown
(Plate 76).

(iii) 'Comtesse du Cayla', deep salmon-pink
blooms with golden reverse (Plate 77).

(iv) 'Mutabilis', an old China hybrid, reminding
one of our modern Floribunda 'Masquerade'. It has
rather large single yellow, pink, and red flowers on
the same truss. Likes a sunny and warm position and
grows to about 4 feet.

R. DAMASCENA, the 'Damask rose'. It is noted for its
scent and many varieties are used for the preparation of
'Attar of Roses'. Recommended varieties are:

(i) *R. damascena* 'Gloire de Guilan'. The pink
blooms are highly scented. The bush has a rather
sprawling habit, although it only grows to about
3 feet.

(ii) 'Mme Hardy'. A sturdy growing bush with
most beautiful blooms, full petalled and of an almost
pure white with a tiny green eye. It is worthy of a
place in any garden.

76. *R. chinensis* 'Bloomfield Abundance'

77. *R. pomifera* var. *duplex*, Wolley-Dods rose

(iii) 'Versicolor' ('York and Lancaster'). A tall-growing tree with blush white and light pink flowers, which though not very shapely are attractive. They may be entirely of one shade or the other, and sometimes are distinctly parti-coloured but never striped as is the case with 'Rosa Mundi' (Plate 78).

R. ECAE. Bright yellow small single flowers on deep red stems, very prickly, 4 to 5 feet.

R. FARRERI, the threepenny-bit rose of Chinese origin. The tall spreading bush is covered with tiny pink flowers the size of the old silver threepenny piece. It is a perfect rose in miniature.

R. FILIPES. China. A good climber, reaching some 20 feet if supported. Loves to ramble over an old thorn tree which has been suitably trimmed. The flowers are borne in large trusses. They are creamy-white and fragrant.

R. GALLICA, or more correctly *R. rubra*, was a religious emblem of the Medes and Persians in the twelfth century. Historically it is probably the oldest of our old roses (Plate 3). Three good varieties are:

78. *R. damascena* 'Versicolor'. The York and Lancaster Rose

(i) 'Belle de Crecy', which although rather straggling in habit is quite an attractive bush. It produces masses of very fragrant pink flowers flecked with violet. It is very effective when planted next to *R. damascena* 'Mme Hardy' described above. Each provides the perfect foil for the other.

(ii) 'Cardinal de Richelieu'. Those who like roses approaching a blue colour will find pleasure in this rather intriguing variety. The bushes are about 3 feet in height and the flowers which open to a deep violet are most effective when the trees are massed in a bed rather than grown as individual specimens.

(iii) 'Versicolor' ('Rosa Mundi'). Large semi-double light crimson blooms striped with pink and white. A bushy tree, about 3 feet high, quite distinct from *R. damascena* 'Versicolor' (Plate 79).

R. HIGHDOWNENSIS. This hybrid of *R. moyesii* was raised by Sir Frederick Stern at Highdown, Sussex. It makes a magnificent shrub with long arching stems covered with single scarlet blooms and, incidentally, with the most vicious thorns. In the autumn it is covered with scarlet, bottle-shaped hips; 8 to 10 feet high.

R. HUGONIS. China. A compact shrub growing to a height of about 6 feet. Its fern-like grey-green foliage makes an excellent background for the small single yellow flowers which cover the shrub in early June.

R. MOSCHATA. A vigorous climber from the Middle East and the Himalayas. It has an enormous covering capacity and will ramble among the branches of trees up to forty feet in height. Control of growth is not easy, and it must be given plenty of room. Its flowers are small single white and are carried in large trusses (Plate 4). In the autumn it is covered with bright red hips. This species has given us that delightful group of hybrid Musks of which the following is a good representative selection, the name of the raiser being given after the varietal name.

Rosa Gallica Versicolor.   *Rosier de France à fleurs panachées.*

79. *R. gallica* 'Versicolor', 'Fair Rosamond's Rose', or *R. gallica*
'Rosa Mundi'. From 'Redouté', *Les Roses*, 1, 135 (1819)

'Berlin', Kordes 1949. Large single blooms, scarlet shaded orange. Blooms are generally in trusses; 4 feet high.

'Bonn', Kordes 1949. A beautiful shrub, whether grown as a specimen bush or massed in larger gardens. Has striking orange-scarlet blooms which are large and fairly full. Is free-flowering and has a delicious musk fragrance.

'Cornelia', Pemberton 1925. Small flowers in large trusses. Apricot and old rose. Very fragrant; 6 feet high.

'Elmshorn', Kordes 1951. Bright crimson. Double flowers borne in small trusses. Light green foliage. Free-flowering and continuing well into the autumn; 6 feet high.

'Felicia', Pemberton 1928. One of the best hybrid musks. Salmon-pink. Fragrant; 6 to 7 feet high.

'Grandmaster', Kordes 1951. Apricot-orange, semi-double flowers borne in trusses.

'Moonlight', Pemberton 1922. Pale cream. Free-flowering in early summer; 5 feet high.

'Pax', Pemberton 1922. Large white flowers with golden stamens. Fragrant; 6 feet high.

'Penelope', Pemberton 1922. Pale salmon-pink fragrant flowers in large trusses. Colour deeper in autumn; 5 feet high (Plate 80).

'Prosperity', Pemberton 1924. Creamy-white in summer but distinctly pink in autumn. Flowers borne in large trusses. Makes a good bush; 5 feet high.

'Vanity', Pemberton 1920. Large single pink fragrant flowers. A beautiful shrub which will reach a height of 8 to 10 feet.

R. MOYESII. This tall shrub (up to 10 feet) has dusky scarlet single flowers with golden stamens. Its bottle-shaped hips of a bright scarlet colour are a joy in the autumn and are of great decorative value (Plates 81 and 16).

80. Hedge of hybrid musk rose 'Penelope'

81. *R. moyesii*

'Nevada'. Often classed as a hybrid of *R. moyesii*, but this is now doubted by some authorities. It is a fine garden shrub with large single white flowers. Free flowering, particularly in June, but it has a good sprinkling of bloom well into the autumn; 7 feet.

R. NITIDA. A dwarf shrub. 2 feet, which should be placed near the front of the shrub garden. It may even be given a place in the rock garden. Very prickly and particularly worth growing for its rich fiery foliage and red hips in the autumn. The flowers are single bright pink.

R. OMEIENSIS var. *pteracantha*. Fern-like foliage. Single white flowers in June. Its great beauty is the very large broad thorns which are only red when young; later they darken in colour. Young stems are most valuable in floral decorations.

R. POMIFERA, the Apple rose, which was introduced from Central Europe. It is a bush about 5 feet in height with single deep pink flowers.

R. pomifera var. *duplex*, Wolley-Dods Rose, is a double form with flowers of a soft pink colour. It will grow to a height of 10 feet, but may be kept small if so desired (Plates 77 and 82).

R. PRIMULA. Turkestan. Small pale yellow flowers on rich red stems. Flowers early. Has beautiful fern-like leaves which on a warm moist evening will fill the air with the most delicious aromatic scent, reminiscent of myrrh; 6 to 7 feet high, but may even reach 10 feet.

R. RUBIGINOSA. 'Eglantine' of Elizabethan times. Known also as 'Sweet Briar'. It is found growing wild in England and its leaves have an apple-like scent. This rose gave us the Penzance briars. The varieties 'Lord Penzance' and 'Lady Penzance' are both subject to black spot. 'Janet's Pride'–white flowers edged with pink–is one of the best varieties to grow.

82. *R. pomifera* var. *duplex*, Wolley-Dods rose

R. RUBRIFOLIA. Central Europe. Worth growing for its foliage alone, which is of an attractive reddish colour and is often sought after by floral decorators. In the autumn its dark cherry-like hips are most attractive. Flowers are small and dark pink.

R. RUGOSA. Japan. Large pink flowers followed by large tomato-coloured hips (Plate 15). These are the hips used in the making of Rose Hip Syrup and are especially rich in vitamin C. The stems are thickly covered with prickly hairs. Owing to the ease with which it throws suckers the *rugosas* make excellent thickets which are almost impenetrable. Two hybrids worthy of a place in the shrub garden are:

(i) 'Blanc Double de Coubert'. Large white, sweetly scented double flowers. The flowers are fleeting, but are quickly followed by others; 6 feet high.

(ii) 'Roseraie de l'Häy'. Probably one of the finest to grow. Very large crimson to mauve flowers. Continuous flowering throughout the summer; 5 to 6 feet high.

R. SPINOSISSIMA. The Scotch briar or Burnet rose. It is found growing wild on the sand dunes of the coast of Great Britain. I have found it on the north Devon coast growing as a small shrubby plant with single yellow flowers. During recent years some of the most beautiful of our shrub roses have resulted from hybridizing varieties of *spinosissima* derivatives with the Hybrid Teas. The following are all beautiful specimens:

'Frühlingsgold' (Spring gold), Kordes 1937. A strong grower, reaching 7 feet in height. The flowers are large semi-double, pale yellow in colour, and of good fragrance (Plate 83).

'Frühlingsmorgen' (Spring morning), Kordes 1942. A beautiful single pale pink with yellow centre, 3 inches across. One of the most attractive shrubs, 6 to 8 feet high.

'Frühlingsanfang' (Spring's opening), Kordes 1950. A strong grower, up to 8 feet, producing very large single yellow flowers in great quantity.

'Frühlingsduft' (Spring fragrance), Kordes 1949. A bush about 4 feet in height producing large numbers of big creamy-yellow flowers.

'Stanwell Perpetual'. Lee 1838. White flowers, fragrant. Grows well in poor soil. A dense shrub up to 5 feet high. In flower during summer and autumn.

83. *R. spinosissima* 'Frühlingsgold'

84. *R. spinosissima* 'Lady Hamilton'. Creamy white flushed rose, reverse white.

R. XANTHINA 'Canary Bird'. It has large single yellow flowers on 6 feet long arching stems and in summer is very floriferous. It is one of the best of the yellow shrub roses (Plate 85).

The shrub roses, which are so different from the Hybrid Teas we are now accustomed to, are becoming increasingly popular. They bring an old-world charm to our modern, more turbulent days and are an echo of the past which is worth preserving. One may say they link the past with the present, and as such they are a most welcome addition to the rose garden of today.

85. *R. xanthina* 'Canary Bird'

CHAPTER 11

EXHIBITING

There is no more enjoyable occupation for the lover of roses than that of exhibiting his perfect blooms at a rose show. In addition to receiving a personal thrill he is able to give joy to those who visit the show, many of whom have no gardens of their own, but who love to see beautiful flowers. Also the rose grower will find that he grows his roses just that little bit better because of the incentive of showing in competition with his fellow rose growers. His own garden becomes more beautiful because he strives to grow perfect blooms.

The first essential for good exhibiting is good cultivation. Each tree must be treated as a potential bearer of show blooms, and by this one does not necessarily mean massive blooms, but perfectly formed ones, free from blemishes and of a size comparable to the best a given variety can produce.

It is not easy, from a small garden, to provide even six blooms which will be in perfect condition at a given hour on a given day in the year, on a show bench which may be several miles away from your garden. How often one hears an exhibitor say his blooms were just a few days too early or too late! But that all lends spice to the adventure.

Advice is sometimes given that pruning of certain varieties should be done so many weeks before a show while other varieties should be pruned at a later date. Unfortunately the vagaries of our climate make exact time-tabling for a living subject almost impossible. Experience will teach you that some varieties will take longer than others for buds to develop and for these buds to open to the perfect flower, but no hard-and-fast rules can be given. It is wise to grow at least six trees of each variety so as to have a reasonable chance of having one or two blooms just right for the day of the show.

Begin exhibiting at your local flower show and do not be too ambitious at first. Study the schedule, select the class you think will suit you best, and be quite sure to comply with the requirements of the particular class. After you have staged your class, watch other more experienced exhibitors staging their blooms, and learn something of the art of exhibiting.

Another year you may be able to transport your blooms to the National Show in London or in the provinces and compete against the best rose exhibitors in the country. Assuming you have given your roses the best care and attention throughout the growing season, there may still be a few matters about which you may require information. What protection must you give your blooms for the two weeks before a show? When must they be cut? How must they be transported to the show? What is the best method to display them? These are all questions which trouble the would-be exhibitor.

PROTECTION OF BLOOMS. Conical bloom protectors clipped on wooden stakes can be used to prevent damage by rain, dew, or sun to blooms which are just beginning to release their petals. The protector should be so arranged that rain falling on it will not drip on the flower and at the same time it must not be so low that the flower will hit the sides if swayed a little by wind. It is sometimes advisable to bend the stem a little and tie it to a stake before putting the protector in position. If the bloom is so near the ground that mud splashes may reach the petals, arrange a second protector upside down underneath the bloom to prevent such damage. It is against the sudden thunderstorm with its accompanying torrential rain which may occur just before a show that provision has to be made. If the weather is dull and

86. Flower buckets in stand to prevent movement

humid but not wet it is advisable to raise the upper protector, otherwise the moist atmosphere in the confined space may cause the petals to rot or cling together.

THE TIME FOR CUTTING. This will depend largely on the distance you have to transport the blooms. If the show is quite near they can be cut in the early morning of the day of the show. If you are showing in bowls or vases cut long stems, remove the lower leaves and thorns, and put them *at once* into a deep container almost full of water. Keep the container in a cool dark place until you are ready to take them to the show. If the show is so far away that you have to make a very early start the roses should be cut the evening before, when the sun is low, and stored in water in a cool place until the morning. Roses to be shown in boxes may be cut with shorter stems and put directly in water in the tubes ready for staging, providing they have not to be transported far. If, however, they have to be taken a long distance by rail or car it is better to cut them with somewhat longer stems and stage them at the show.

TRANSPORTING BLOOMS TO THE SHOW. Again the method used will vary according to the distance the blooms have to travel. If possible it is by far the best to keep the stems in water from the moment they are cut to the time they are displayed on the show bench.

Two methods I have found useful in taking the blooms up to 200 miles by road are shown in the illustrations (Plates 86 and 87). The home-made container with three flower buckets (or large metal cans) will carry sixty blooms (twenty in each container) and will ride quite well at the back of the car with the seat removed. The stems should be tied with raffia just below the flowers, to prevent rubbing, and the flowers should be covered with tissue paper. It is important that the flowers are dry when packed. When this method is used it is well to travel by night if a journey of 200 miles is contemplated. The second method gives more protection and is one I have used for many years. The boxes can easily be made

87. Showing box lined with tissue paper lying flat ready for packing. There are two rows of five tubes in each half of the box

by a handy-man by first making a completely closed box, and then sawing it through the middle longitudinally. The two halves are then hinged together (Plate 87) and small hooks fixed to keep the box closed. Ventilation holes should be bored near the top and a leather strap arranged to serve as a handle. Inside the two halves, shelves suitably bored to carry bloom holders are placed at the required height and screw-eyes fixed so that the stems may be tied in position. To pack this box place it flat on the floor, with the tubes empty, and line it with tissue paper, allowing an overhang to cover the blooms. Before packing Hybrid Tea-type roses it is advisable to wrap each bloom lightly in tissue paper which is twisted above the bloom to make a kind of bag. Each tube will take two or three stems and the whole box will carry forty to sixty blooms. The stems must reach the bottom of the tubes, and when packed string or raffia should be tied across the stems, using the screw-eyes for this purpose. The box can now be stood upright and the tubes filled with water.

Floribunda varieties are packed in the same way but the heads are not wrapped in tissue paper. It is advisable to remove the points of the thorns to prevent possible tearing of foliage during packing and unpacking. When packed in this way the roses travel well by rail or car. The Hybrid Tea-type roses should be packed when the outer petals only are just beginning to reflex. Large exhibition blooms may be tied with thick soft wool to hold the inner petals in place and avoid damage by vibration during the journey, but it is useless to tie the thinner decorative varieties as these will almost certainly shatter when the wool is removed. It is better to pack these varieties when the outer petals are just beginning to leave the bud; they will grow during the journey.

STAGING THE BLOOMS. Try to be at the show in good time; there is nothing so worrying to an exhibitor as a feeling of being rushed. Unpack the blooms and put

88. Prize-winning box of six roses

89. Prize-winning bowl of rose 'Ethel Sanday'

90. Prize-winning bowl of eighteen roses

the stems in water at once. If you have several classes to stage, it is helpful to have the varieties you intend to show in each class in separate containers. Have all materials for staging handy: secateurs, scissors, camel-hair brush, wire (if wiring is allowed), rushes or other suitable material, e.g. lonicera, cut to the required lengths for vases, labels for naming the roses, a small watering-can with long spout for filling rose tubes or topping up the vases; then set to work in a calm, methodical manner.

STAGING IN BOWLS OR VASES. Be careful to use bowls or vases of the size indicated in the schedule. Pack the rushes in the vases before you fill them up with water. Select the roses you wish to display and arrange them so that they show to best advantage, e.g. in a vase of mixed varieties do not have two roses of one colour next to each other if it can be avoided.

Some excellent roses have a bad habit of 'nodding their heads'; these should be wired (unless the regulations forbid it, and then such roses should be excluded). Wiring is not difficult if done carefully, but a little practice is necessary. Most exhibitors will have to admit having 'beheaded' a bloom when wiring is first attempted, and if it is one of the best or the only one left of a required variety the effect is certainly disturbing.

TO WIRE A ROSE. Using first finger and thumb of the left hand, take a firm hold of the seed receptacle just below the outer petal. Hold the wire fairly close to the end to be inserted and push it gently but firmly into the seed receptacle. Wind the lower half of the wire round the stem and the process is complete. Special wires nine and twelve inches long may be bought from horticultural sundriesmen. The beginner will find it helpful to sharpen the end of the wire with a small file before insertion.

When arranging a bowl be careful to find out if it is to be judged for all-round effect or for frontal effect only. Try to arrange the blooms so that there are no big gaps between them and bring out the colour effect by a judicious mixing of colours.

Good clean foliage will greatly enhance the beauty of the blooms.

STAGING BOX CLASSES. These classes are principally for the display of large, well-formed exhibition blooms. Special boxes and tubes fitted with bloom holders are required. The rose stem is passed through the ring at the top of the bloom holder, then through the smaller one lower down until the bloom fits snugly on the ring, its sepals being arranged above the ring so as to support the outer petals; the stem is then wired to the upright support. The tubes at the back should be raised, those in the second row raised to a lesser degree, and those in the front row not raised at all. The back of the box is also raised by using the metal supports supplied with the box. Before the blooms are put into the box the spaces between the rose tubes should be covered with moss to give a green background for the roses staged. When staging is completed insert the name slips in the holders attached to the tubes.

DRESSING BLOOMS. Some exhibitors make a habit of removing any damaged outside petals, and then hide the defect by pressing down the next row of petals. Personally, I dislike this practice as I feel it is far better to protect the rose from weather and show it in its completeness. The object of dressing a rose is not to hide defects, but by opening the petals to reveal the beauty and depth of colour on the inside of the petal. This may be done by using a camel-hair brush to depress a petal, at the same time supporting the base of the petal by the forefinger of the left hand. It can also be done by gently taking hold of the centre of the base of the outer petals in turn between the finger and thumb of the right hand, exerting a little pressure and moving the finger and thumb gently upwards, slightly turning the wrist at the same time so as to move the petals outwards. The next row of petals should be treated similarly, but to a lesser extent. Much practice will be required when using this method to get a result resembling the natural opening of the flower, and it will soon be realized that a flower must be in the right stage of growth before 'dressing' can be carried out. Nothing looks more unlike a natural bloom than one which has been overdressed, leaving the rose with its outer petals standing out horizontally and a tight cone of inner petals resting on them. Always remember an overdressed bloom is a bad bloom in the eyes of a competent judge.

STAGING FLORIBUNDA CLASSES. These classes are becoming increasingly popular and with the wide range of varieties now available make very attractive exhibits. It is essential to have a large number of blooms fully open on the spray, and one can be assured of this by removing at an early stage the largest centre buds and a few of the smaller buds from each spray. This will leave a large number of equal-sized buds which will open to give a head well filled with fully opened blooms. They travel well and will remain fresh for many hours. The buds of some varieties open slowly in water, and consequently the head should have many fully opened blooms before cutting.

CHAPTER 12

A SELECT LIST OF ROSES

For the benefit of those who wish to make a quick selection of roses of a particular colour I have placed some eighty varieties of good-growing Hybrid Tea-type roses of which I have personal experience, in seven main colour groups: reds, pinks, yellows, whites or creams, bicolours, coppery-orange shades, shades of lavender. Lists of Floribundas and Climbing and Rambling roses are also included.

The depth of colour and the shade varies considerably in the various groups, and reference should be made to the detailed description of each variety. This is not meant to be a comprehensive list, but it is representative of the best roses in commerce today. For more extensive lists the reader is referred to the Select List of Roses published by the National Rose Society.

Reds

BACCHUS (Dickson 1953). Bright scarlet, free flowering, hardy, and of erect habit. Fragrant. Good foliage but somewhat subject to mildew on heavy land.

BADEN-BADEN (Kordes 1954). Rich deep red. Fragrant and very free flowering. High centred and moderately vigorous.

BLOODSTONE (McGredy 1949). Coral red. Not very pronounced fragrance. Flowers borne on long stems. Good foliage.

BRILLIANT (Kordes 1952). Deep scarlet. Large well-shaped fragrant blooms. Vigorous grower. Dark green foliage. A fine rose, but apt to 'blue'.

CHARLES MALLERIN (Meilland 1951). A very deep

91. Rose 'Ena Harkness'

velvety red and extremely fragrant rose. Not always a good shape and does not stand up to frost very well.

CRIMSON GLORY (Kordes 1935). Velvety crimson. Gives large blooms of good shape, but fades to an uninteresting brown colour. Highly scented. Needs good cultivation.

DR F. G. CHANDLER (Dickson 1938). Deep scarlet-crimson. Large blooms of very good form. Very fragrant. Responds well to good cultivation.

ENA HARKNESS (Norman 1946) (Plate 91). Rich crimson-scarlet. Beautifully formed flowers which do not fade. Fragrant. One of the best garden varieties, but does not do so well on very heavy land. When the soil suits it there are few more rewarding roses.

ÉTOILE DE HOLLANDE (Verschuren 1919). Deep crimson and highly scented. An old favourite, but there are better reds today. Its blooms open rather flat and the foliage is somewhat sparse.

FANDANGO (Swim 1950). Scarlet, shaded orange. An arresting colour. Produces large flowers, but they are rather thin and open. Fragrant. Growth vigorous and upright.

JOSEPHINE BRUCE (Bees 1949). Deep velvety crimson. One of the most beautiful of the dark reds. Produces large fragrant blooms which last well when cut. Most attractive foliage.

KARL HERBST (Kordes 1950). Deep crimson with somewhat lighter reverse. Large, full, well-shaped flowers. A perfect grower with excellent foliage. Blooms need protection against wet. Is best in a dry season, but always worth growing.

KONRAD ADENAUER (Tantau 1954). Dark crimson. Large and very fragrant blooms. A vigorous grower.

MME LOUISE LAPERRIÈRE (Laperrière 1952). This seedling of 'Crimson Glory' has the deep scarlet colour of its parent. It is very fragrant and is a fine bedding variety.

92. Rose 'Eden Rose'

POINSETTIA (Howard and Smith 1938). Bright scarlet.
Blooms light up in artificial light. A first-class bloom
so far as shape and colour are concerned, but it has
no scent. A vigorous upright grower.

RED ENSIGN (Norman 1947). Deep crimson. A well-
formed rose of rich fragrance. A very vigorous
grower and a perfect bloom for the exhibitor.

WILLIAM HARVEY (Norman 1948). Scarlet crimson
with velvety texture of petal. Large, well-formed
and fragrant blooms, but petals are apt to come with
a frilled edge. A good rose for the exhibitor.

Pinks

ANNE LETTS (Letts 1954). Pale pink with somewhat
paler reverse. Large fragrant blooms of good shape.
Glossy foliage. A first-class modern variety.

CHARLOTTE ARMSTRONG (Lammerts 1940). Deep
pink with a touch of yellow at the base of the petals.
Slightly fragrant. Vigorous and very free flowering.
Does not mind wet.

COMTESSE VANDAL (Leenders 1932). Pale salmon-pink with a tinge of coppery colour on the reverse. Free flowering. A first-class garden and decorative variety.

DOROTHY ANDERSON (McGredy 1949). Rose-pink which fades rather quickly as the blooms open. A very large, well-formed rose and a vigorous grower. Needs much disbudding.

EDEN ROSE (Meilland 1953) (Plate 92). Brilliant carmine with lighter reverse. A truly magnificent rose. Highly disease-resistant foliage of rich green colour. Very vigorous.

ELAINE (Robinson 1950). Pink, large well-shaped blooms. Very susceptible to wet. A rose for the exhibitor.

JUNE PARK (Bertram Park 1958). A highly scented rich deep pink rose. Very vigorous. An excellent garden variety.

LADY SYLVIA (Stevens 1927). This sport from Mme Butterfly is a beautiful soft pink with yellow shadings. Richly scented. A good grower and very free flowering. Splendid for cut flowers if disbudded.

LA JOLLA (Swim 1955). Salmon-pink with touches of yellow. Large light-centred blooms. Fragrant. Its colour is somewhat different from any other pink. Dark glossy foliage.

LAL (Easlea 1933). Two shades of pink, the outer side of the petal being much deeper than the inner. Highly scented and of good shape. Rather subject to die-back.

MARGARET (Alex Dickson 1955). Bright china pink, slightly shaded yellow. Very fragrant. Vigorous and free flowering. One of the most beautiful pink roses ever produced, but needs protection during a very wet season.

MICHELE MEILLAND (Meilland 1945). Soft salmon pink, well formed and slightly fragrant blooms.

MONIQUE (Paolino 1949) (Plate 93). Deep pink, very fragrant and free flowering. Is a vigorous grower.

93. Rose 'Monique'

PERFECTA (Kordes 1957). Ivory ground richly shaded with carmine. A perfectly formed flower. Vigorous grower with rich glossy green foliage. A wonderful rose particularly beautiful in the autumn.

PICTURE (McGredy 1932). Just what its name suggests! A lovely clear rose-pink. When fully open looks like a pink gardenia. Light green foliage and highly resistant to disease. As near as possible the perfect garden rose.

PINK CHARMING (Leenders 1952). Pale pink, rather loose blooms when fully open. Fragrant. Good uniform growth. Blooms not affected by wet.

PINK SPIRAL (McGredy 1952). Deep rose-pink. Large blooms of spiral formation. A good grower with large grey-green foliage.

SHOT SILK (Alex Dickson 1924). Makes a really gay bed of shades of pink and yellow which is still hard to equal. It fades rather quickly, but not to an unpleasant colour. Very fragrant. Likes a cool climate and is seen at its best in the north of England. Foliage a rich, glossy green. In spite of its age it is still a rose to grow.

SHOW GIRL (Lammerts 1946). Deep rose-pink. Produces large blooms of very good shape. Fades a little in sun and is liable to damage by wet. Vigorous growth. An excellent rose for the exhibitor if protected from wet and sun in the opening stage.

SUZON LOTTHÉ (Meilland 1947). The palest of pale pinks with a slightly deeper pink edging. Highly scented. Tall and vigorous but suffers badly in a wet season when the blooms are completely ruined.

THE DOCTOR (Howard and Smith 1936) (Plate 94). A pure pink. Very highly scented. Large well-formed blooms. Must be pruned lightly to get good growth. Blooms well in autumn.

VERSCHUREN'S PINK (Verschuren 1948). A glistening rose-pink with deeper shadings. Large blooms which are apt to split if grown strongly. The best-shaped

94. Rose 'The Doctor'

blooms are on the thinner shoots and are best in the autumn. Damaged by wet.

VIOLINISTA COSTA (Camprubi-Nadal 1936). Rosy salmon with orange shading. Glossy leathery foliage. An excellent bedding rose which does not mind wet. Blooms open rather flat. Very vigorous growth.

WILLIAM MOORE (McGredy 1935). Deep pink and well-formed flowers. Slight fragrance. Fairly vigorous. A good exhibition rose.

Yellows

BARBARA RICHARDS (Alex Dickson 1930). Maize-yellow. Very large and full, well-shaped flowers. Richly scented. Looks well when cut. Moderately vigorous. Responds well to good cultivation.

BUCCANEER (Swim 1953). Buttercup-yellow. Tea fragrance. Tall, erect, extra-vigorous grower. A very good garden variety.

DIAMOND JUBILEE (Boerner, Jackson, and Perkins 1947). Buff-yellow, sometimes rather paler. Large full blooms. Dark leathery foliage. Very free flowering.

DIRECTEUR GUERIN (Gaujard 1935). Creamy-yellow with much deeper shadings in the centre. In the autumn it is almost buff yellow. Very large blooms which must be protected against the wet.

ELLINOR LE GRICE (Le Grice 1949). A pure yellow rose. Somewhat globular in form. Very free flowering and vigorous. A good garden rose.

ETHEL SANDAY (Oliver Mee 1953) (Plate 89). Yellow with tinges of apricot, somewhat paler on some soils. Large blooms of perfect shape. Slightly fragrant. Very free flowering.

GOLDEN DAWN (Grant 1929). Clear pale yellow. Slight tea scent. Beautiful foliage. An excellent bedding rose, but apt to give split blooms unless lightly pruned.

GOLDEN MELODY (Pedro Dot 1934). Light buff-yellow, sometimes paler. A good decorative rose

95. Rose 'Grand'mère Jenny'

with long stems, but can produce large blooms. Vigorous growth.

GRAND'MÈRE JENNY (Meilland 1950) (Plate 95). Yellow, shaded with pink. Large, long, pointed blooms. Fragrant. Vigorous and free flowering. Does not mind wet.

LADY BELPER (Verschuren 1948). Light orange-yellow. Slight fragrance. Blooms are of good shape and substance. Vigorous. Dark glossy foliage. One of the best of its colour.

MARCEL GRET (Meilland 1947). Chrome yellow. Long pointed buds but rather thin and opens very quickly to rather poor blooms. Vigorous growth.

McGREDY'S YELLOW (McGredy 1933). Bright pure yellow. Large, perfectly formed blooms. Does not mind wet. Vigorous growth. It is still one of the very best yellows.

MOONBEAM (Robinson 1950). Pale yellow – deeper colour in the autumn. Large, high-centred blooms. Foliage susceptible to black spot and must be sprayed early. Does not stand up to wet weather, but is an excellent rose in a dry season.

PEACE (Meilland 1942). Colour varies from light to deep yellow with pink edging on petals. Very large and well-shaped blooms. Extremely vigorous and free flowering. Does not mind wet. It is hard to find fault with this rose, which has rightly been described as 'the rose of the century'.

PHYLLIS GOLD (Robinson 1934). Rich yellow, particularly on the side shoots, where the blooms are smaller. Always a good shape. Vigorous grower but rather sprawling in habit.

SAM McGREDY (McGredy 1937). Cream to buff yellow. Very large blooms of exquisite shape, having a spirally formed centre. Does not mind wet. Light pruning and good cultivation produce vigorous free-flowering trees.

SIR HENRY SEGRAVE (Alex Dickson 1932). Pale

96. Vase of Rose 'Sir Henry Segrave'

lemon-yellow. Every flower is of perfect shape. Vigorous grower with attractive foliage. Liable to damage by wet, but is exquisite in a dry season or if protected in the opening stages (Plate 96).

SPEK'S YELLOW (Verschuren-Pechtold 1948). Rich golden yellow. Small but well-shaped flowers. Slight fragrance. Vigorous grower. Glossy foliage. Does not mind wet. A capital garden rose.

SUTTER'S GOLD (Swim 1949). Golden yellow with shadings of pink on the outside of the petals. Fragrant. Long stems with good foliage.

ULSTER MONARCH (McGredy 1949). Rich creamy buff. Large, high-pointed blooms. Not very vigorous growth, but produces excellent blooms.

Whites and Creams

BRIDAL ROBE (McGredy 1953). Ivory-white. Vigorous. Produces large flowers of good shape. Excellent under glass, not a good garden variety.

MCGREDY'S IVORY (McGredy 1929). Creamy-white. Long pointed bud, large petals. Flowers are of good size, but are liable to damage by wet. One of the best of the whites.

MESSAGE (Meilland 1956) (Plate 97). White with greenish shading at base of petals. Free flowering. Fragrant. Blooms not very large.

MRS CHARLES LAMPLOUGH (McGredy 1920). White with a touch of cream when bloom is young. Fairly vigorous growth. Foliage rather small. An exhibitor's rose which must be protected from wet.

REX ANDERSON (McGredy 1938). Rich deep cream with a touch of yellow at the base of the petals. Slight fragrance. Straggling growth. Not a good garden variety, but indispensable to the exhibitor. Produces large flowers of good shape.

VIRGO (Mallerin 1947) (Plate 98). Pure white. Medium sized, high pointed blooms which hold their shape

97. Rose 'Message'

98. Rose 'Virgo'

well. Free flowering. Good for cutting. Not so easily damaged by wet as other whites usually are.

FRAU KARL DRUSCHKI (Lammerts 1901). Hybrid Perpetual. Pure white. Buds are touched with pink on the outer petals. No fragrance but has large well-formed blooms. Very vigorous and like most hybrid perpetuals should not be pruned hard. An old variety, but still one of the best of the whites. Makes an excellent shrub or standard.

Bicolours

CLEOPATRA (Kordes 1956). Deep scarlet on inside and yellow on outside of the petals. Very little fragrance. Best as a maiden.

CONDESA DE SASTAGO (Pedro Dot 1933). Red on inside and yellow on outside. Full flat blooms which are apt to split. Bright glossy foliage.

GAY CRUSADER (Robinson 1948). Orange-scarlet on inside, deep yellow on outside of the petals. Large blooms of well-shaped flowers with pointed centre. Moderately vigorous. A good bedder.

SULTANE (Meilland 1946). Vermilion on the inside with golden yellow on the outside of the petals. Medium sized blooms. Does not hold its shape well.

TZIGANE (Meilland 1949) (Plate 99). Velvety scarlet on inside with yellow on the outside of the petals. An upright grower with rich, glossy foliage.

Coppery Orange and Orange-red Shades

FLAMING SUNSET (Eddie 1947). Shades of orange and yellow. A good bedder. Light green foliage.

MARY WHEATCROFT (Robinson 1945). Bright coppery-red. Medium sized blooms. Fragrant. Free flowering, dark bronze-green foliage. An attractive rose in the garden.

MRS SAM MCGREDY (McGredy 1929). One of the earliest roses of its colour, coppery orange-salmon,

99. Rose 'Tzigane'

and in cool climates is still one of the best. The blooms are of excellent shape and are borne on long stems. The early foliage is bright bronze-red, but it darkens later in the season. A most attractive garden rose which is often quite large.

MME HENRI GUILLOT (Mallerin 1938). Brilliant orange-red. Large well-formed blooms which open rather quickly and fade to a much lighter colour. Rich, glossy, and large foliage. A glorious patch of colour in the garden.

PRINCESS MARINA (Robinson 1935). Similar to 'Mrs Sam McGredy' but lighter in colour. Moderately vigorous but not very free flowering.

SIGNORA (Aicardi 1936). Flame-red with orange. A good grower. Blooms are of good shape and are fragrant. A good rose for cutting.

Shades of Lavender

GREY PEARL (McGredy 1944). Lavender-grey with brownish shadings. Rather globular flowers. Vigorous growth. Useful for decorative arrangements.

LILAC TIME (McGredy 1955). Light lavender-lilac. Well formed and slightly fragrant. Free flowering. Good grower. Does not easily fade.

PRELUDE (Meilland 1945). Lavender with a touch of mauve. Small flowers. Moderate growth.

ROYAL TAN (McGredy 1955). Purplish-violet with brownish base. Medium sized blooms. Good for decorative work.

Floribunda Roses

I have selected forty varieties of which I have personal knowledge, all are vigorous in growth with good foliage, and unless otherwise stated make large heads of bloom. They provide masses of colour from June until the frosts put an end to their gaiety. Again they are classed roughly according to colour.

100. Rose 'Frensham'

Reds

ALAIN (Meilland 1948). Carmine-red. Semi-double.

BORDER KING (De Ruiter 1950). Bright crimson.

COCORICO (Meilland 1950). Bright scarlet with darker scarlet shading. Semi-double.

DONALD PRIOR (Prior 1934). Deep crimson scarlet. Apt to give single blooms on a stem at the first blooming.

DUSKY MAIDEN (Le Grice 1947). Dark maroon-scarlet with golden anthers. Single.

FIRECRACKER (Boerner, Jackson, and Perkins 1955). Orange-scarlet with yellow at base.

FRENSHAM (Norman 1946) (Plate 100). Deep scarlet crimson, exceptionally vigorous. One of the best.

HIGHLIGHT (Robinson 1957). Vivid flame scarlet, large clusters. Apt to be damaged by wet. Vigorous grower.

KAREN POULSEN (Poulsen 1933). Scarlet. Single.

KORONA (Kordes 1954). Brilliant orange-scarlet.

MOULIN ROUGE (Meilland 1952). Scarlet. Lasts well.

RED FAVOURITE (Tantau 1951) (Plate 101). Scarlet-crimson, rich dark colour. Really good. Rather dwarf habit.

RED WONDER (De Ruiter 1955). Rich crimson. Large blooms in clusters.

SHEPHERD'S DELIGHT (Alex Dickson & Sons 1958). A glorious colour with shades of orange and red. Large trusses of semi-double flowers. A strong grower with a long flowering period (illustrated on the cover).

SIREN (Kordes 1952). Orange-scarlet. Large blooms in clusters.

Pinks

BETTY PRIOR (Prior 1935). Carmine with light pink reverse. Single.

CECILE BRUNNER (hybrid china) (Ducher 1880). Flesh pink. Perfectly formed roses in miniature, giving good clusters.

101. Rose 'Red Favourite'

CHARMING MAID (Le Grice 1953). Pink, shaded gold. Gives single blooms on stems until well established, when it gives good heads of large single blooms. A beautiful variety.

DAINTY MAID (Le Grice 1938). Two shades of pink, pale inside and deeper on the outside. Golden anthers. One of the best of its colour.

ELSE POULSEN (Poulsen 1924). Rose-pink. Semi-double. Subject to mildew.

MÄRCHENLAND (Tantau 1952) (Plates 39–43). Pale pink with somewhat deeper reverse.

PINOCCHIO (Kordes 1940). Pale pink with salmon shading. Each individual bloom is like a small Hybrid Tea type.

POULSEN'S BEDDER (Poulsen 1948). Rose-pink. Double blooms in small clusters.

POULSEN'S PINK (Poulsen 1939). Bright pink shaded gold.

QUEEN ELIZABETH (Lammerts 1955). Pure clear pink. Each individual bloom is a small Hybrid Tea type and is well shaped. Blooms are carried in long-stemmed clusters. An excellent variety and a very strong grower.

ROSEMARY ROSE (De Ruiter 1954). Unique in form. Light crimson large flowers, opening rather flat.

RUDOLPH TIMM (Kordes 1951). Pale pink with deeper pink edging. Semi-double. Very large head of bloom.

Salmon

BORDER QUEEN (De Ruiter 1951). Salmon-pink suffused with orange-red. A beautiful and unusual colour. A lovely garden variety, but does not last when cut.

FASHION (Boerner, Jackson, and Perkins 1947) (Plate 102). Subject to rust in some places.

SALMON PERFECTION (De Ruiter 1952). Dark salmon. Medium-sized individual blooms. Semi-double. Globular in shape.

VOGUE (Boerner, Jackson, and Perkins 1949). Deep salmon-pink. Large well-formed blooms.

102. Rose 'Fashion'

Yellows

ALLGOLD (Le Grice 1956). Deep unfading yellow. Free growing, ideal bedder.

GOLDEN FLEECE (Boerner, Jackson, and Perkins 1956). A very promising yellow. Very free flowering.

GOLDILOCKS (Boerner, Jackson, and Perkins 1945). Deep yellow which fades quickly in sun. Makes a dwarf, bushy plant.

SUNDANCE (Poulsen 1953). Clear yellow in bud, but shaded pink and orange when open. Rather charming.

SUNNY MAID (Fletcher 1949). Bright sulphur-yellow. Fades rather quickly and is apt to give only one or two blooms on a stem until several years old. When established produces good heads of large single flowers, particularly in autumn. Most attractive.

YELLOWHAMMER (McGredy 1954). Deep golden yellow. Does not fade quite so easily as other yellows.

Whites

GLACIER (Boerner, Jackson, and Perkins 1952). Large, full individual flowers. Does not like wet.

IRENE OF DENMARK (Poulsen 1949) (Plate 103). Medium sized individual blooms, making a large head. Very free flowering and one of the earliest in bloom.

YVONNE RABIER (Turbat 1910). Small flowers but very large clusters. Very vigorous, good enough for a hedge or large specimen bush.

Others worthy of mention which do not fit any of the above groups are:

CIRCUS (Swim 1956). Yellow changing to pink and red. Big clusters. Very vigorous and bushy.

FAUST (Kordes 1956). Very strong plant with beautiful yellow flowers, slightly flushed with red, of the hybrid tea type. An excellent variety.

LAVENDER PINOCCHIO (Boerner, Jackson, and Perkins

103. Rose 'Irene of Denmark'

1948). Chocolate brown to pink bud. Flower opens
to a smoky lavender with yellow anthers. Unique.

MASQUERADE (Boerner, Jackson, and Perkins 1948)
(Plate 104). Opens to clear yellow and as the flower
ages turns to pink and finally red. As all the individual flowers do not open at once it is possible to have
all three colours in the cluster at the same time. It
makes quite a gay bed and is very free flowering.

Climbing and Rambling Roses

The following list of twenty-two of varying types will
give ample choice for a medium-sized garden.

Summer Flowering Ramblers

ALBERIC BARBIER (Barbier 1900). Deep yellow buds,
but flowers fade to creamy-white. Large clusters.
Flowers in June. Fragrant. Suitable for arch, pergola, screen, or north wall. Glossy foliage.

ALBERTINE (Barbier 1921). Reddish-salmon buds.
Coppery-orange flowers. Very fragrant. One of the
most rewarding of the ramblers. Suitable for arch or
pergola.

AMERICAN PILLAR (Dr W. van Fleet 1902). Bright
rose-red with white eye. Large clusters. An old
favourite for arch, pergola, or pillar.

CRIMSON SHOWER (Norman 1951). Crimson. Large
semi-double flowers borne in trusses. Makes a good
pillar (Plates 46 and 47) and is very beautiful from
July to September.

DR W. VAN FLEET (Dr W. van Fleet 1910). Soft bluish-
pink. Very free flowering in July. Fragrant. Suitable
for arch, pergola, north and east walls (Plates 44 and
45). Will do well in towns.

DOROTHY PERKINS (Jackson and Perkins 1901). Rose-
pink, large clusters. An old favourite for pillar, arch,
or pergola. Makes a good weeping standard.

104. Rose 'Masquerade'

Perpetual Flowering Climbers

CORAL DAWN (Boerner, Jackson, and Perkins 1952). A lovely deep coral pink, fragrant, a good pillar rose.

DANSE DU FEU (Mallerin 1954). Makes a lovely pillar rose and blooms until November. Does not mind wet in the least. An excellent variety.

GUINÉE (Mallerin 1938). Very dark scarlet. Large well-formed, very fragrant flowers. Covers a wall very quickly.

MEG (Gossett 1955). Pink with yellow shadings. Large, semi-double blooms. A lovely rose for a pillar.

MERMAID (Paul 1918). Clear primrose yellow with deep orange stamens. Glossy foliage. Continuous flowering. One of the best of the Climbers.

MME ALFRED CARRIÈRE (Schwartz 1879) (Plate 105). A descendant of the original Noisette rose. A vigorous climber but not very hardy. It is very pale pink, almost white. Suitable for a wall facing south. Although an old rose, it is still one of the very best.

THE NEW DAWN (Dreer 1930). Delicate soft pink. A perpetual flowering sport of 'Dr W. van Fleet,' to which it is very similar in form and colour.

ZÉPHIRINE DROUHIN (Bizot 1868). Bright carmine-pink. Very fragrant. Thornless. Flowers in July with some blooms again in the autumn. Covers a wall or shed (Plate 52).

Large Flowered Climbers and Climbing Sports

The former are mainly summer flowering, but they give a certain number of autumn blooms. The climbing sports are best grown on walls.

CHAPLIN'S PINK (Chaplin 1929). Soft pink. Semi-double large blooms with golden yellow anthers. A vigorous grower for arch, pergola, pillar, and south or west walls.

CL. CRIMSON GLORY (Miller 1941). Climbing sport of the dwarf variety. Deep scarlet, better blooms than the parent. Gives some autumn blooms.

105. Climbing rose 'Mme Alfred Carrière' at Sissinghurst Castle, Kent

CL. ÉTOILE DE HOLLANDE (Leenders 1932). Climbing sport. Bright scarlet crimson, highly scented blooms.

CL. GOLDEN DAWN (Le Grice 1947). Climbing sport which gives better shaped blooms than the parent. They are less inclined to split.

CL. GOLDEN OPHELIA (Hage 1924). Climbing sport. Rich golden yellow paler at the edges. Produces a good crop of bloom in the autumn when grown on a wall with a south-east aspect.

CL. MRS SAM McGREDY (Wilson 1947). Climbing sport. Deep salmon. A lovely climber which makes a grand show on a wall or pillar. Gives better blooms than its parent in warmer climates.

PAUL'S SCARLET CLIMBER (Paul 1915). Bright scarlet crimson. Semi-double flowers in clusters. An old favourite for piilar, arch, or east wall.

PAUL'S LEMON PILLAR (Paul 1915). Pale lemon-yellow. Gives large exhibition blooms, very full and fragrant. Grows well on pillar, wall, or screen. Flowers only once – in June or early July.

CHAPTER 13

A MONTH-TO-MONTH REMINDER FOR THE ROSE GROWER

October

THIS is a convenient month to start the rose year, provided you have *already ordered* your new trees. If you have not done this there is no time to lose – you may even now find that the very varieties you want are sold out. Now is the time to finish the preparation of new rose beds. If you are merely replacing individual trees in an already planted bed it is well to dig out the old soil from as large an area as possible, without damaging neighbouring trees and replace it by new soil. Before filling in the holes with the new soil, dig the second spit well and introduce some well-rotted manure or compost plus bone meal. The newly prepared sites for replacements should now be left until next month or later so that the soil will have time to settle.

Time may be given to tidying existing beds, collecting and burning fallen leaves, and the final hoeing of the surface soil.

Trees may be lifted from the garden, root pruned, and potted for cultivation under glass (see Chapter 9). Established pot roses which have been standing out of doors since July should be top dressed and the pots examined for worms. If repotting is necessary, now is the time to do it. Towards the end of the month they may be brought into the cold greenhouse.

November

This is the month when new trees, if ordered early, will arrive. Planting may be done any time from now until the end of March, provided the soil is in a suitable condition. A dry October means good planting conditions in November, provided the planting can be done before the rains make the soil sticky. On heavy soils I find it often pays to delay planting until March unless the weather in October and November is exceptionally dry. Continue tidying-up operations and shorten the long stems of established trees so that they will not be blown about by the wind. In parts of the country where hard frost is expected, earthing up the trees some five or six inches will prevent many losses. A sprinkling of bone meal, which is very slow acting, hoed in the beds in the early part of the month, aids spring growth.

Pot roses not brought into the greenhouse in October should be dealt with without further delay.

December

Planting may be continued if weather conditions are suitable. Standard briars cut from the hedgerows should be planted. Protect trees 'heeled in' by covering with straw or sacking.

Prune rose trees under glass towards the end of the month.

January

Read as much rose literature as you can, and think of future plans for the garden. Join the National Rose Society if you have not already done so. If in an area subject to black spot, etc., spray the beds and trees with Buisol. It is well to look over any trees on screens, pergolas, or poles and see that the stems are well tied to the supports.

About the middle of the month a little artificial heat may be required in the greenhouse to maintain 45°F. Ventilators should be kept open. When trees begin to break into leaf spray with clean water at the temperature of the house.

February

Prune Floribundas. Spray beds and trees with Buisol if not done in January. If no frost, about the middle of the month head back stocks budded in July. Insert canes at once; at this stage they will indicate the position of the budded stocks and later the new shoots must be tied to them. Maintain the temperature of the greenhouse within the range of 60°F. (day) and 45°F. (night).

March

Use any suitable opportunity for planting trees not planted in the autumn. Prune these trees before planting – it saves stooping! Watch for growth on established Hybrid Tea trees and begin pruning *as soon as* growth starts. In case of keen frost it is better to delay pruning until early April, but if your roses are required for the end of June it is safer to finish pruning by the first day of spring.

After pruning burn all stems cut off and scatter the ash over the beds. Follow the cultural operations given in Chapter 6. Now is the time to give a good mulch of farm-yard manure; hoe the beds thoroughly before applying the mulch.

Daily spraying of pot roses is essential. A little liquid Derris in the water will protect from greenfly. Day temperature 70°F., night 60°F.

Don't forget the weekly waterings with the mixture suggested in Chapter 9.

April

Finish all pruning as soon as possible, carrying out cultural operations as described above. Spray all trees with Buisol (rust) and Orthocide (black spot); see pp. 86-7. Check over all staked trees (standards, etc.) and renew ties and stakes where necessary.

Pot plants will require much care and attention this month. Some form of shading is necessary at midday.

Look out for caterpillars. Watch ventilators to avoid an attack of mildew. If any mildew appears spray at once with Karathane or dust with green sulphur. Maintain a moist atmosphere in the house by watering the path between the staging. Endeavour to keep the temperature between 75°F. (day) and 65°F. (night).

May

Watch for greenfly and caterpillars out of doors, and deal with them according to instructions in Chapter 7. Give a further spraying with Buisol and Orthocide. Thin out the poor growths at the base of the tree, as these simply serve as harbourers of insect pests. Put lawn mowings on beds. Scatter them thinly and use hoe or cultivator to prevent any matting together. Keep down weeds by hoeing as often as possible. If weather is dry apply overhead watering once a week.

Pot roses may be removed from the house as soon as they have finished blooming.

June

Continue hoeing beds. Give overhead watering if continuous dry weather. Disbud. Feed trees either by fertilizers dissolved in water or by scattering on beds and watering in (see Chapter 6). Begin to think of your local or the National Show. Write for schedules if not already done so, study them, get all things ready which you will want for the show (see Chapter 11). Don't forget to enter in time.

Rugosa standards should be budded this month if possible.

Pot roses will be ready for putting outside in their summer quarters. Thoroughly clean greenhouse as soon as it is empty. Give the trees an occasional watering in dry weather.

July

This is the month to enjoy your rose garden; it will probably never be better. Cut roses carefully down to a suitable eye. Remove dead heads, again cutting down to an outgrowing eye, the first or second below the dead flower. Don't overdo long cutting on any one tree. Small applications of fertilizers may be applied once a fortnight until mid-August, but then these should cease.

Budding should be carried out as soon as the stocks are ready. Remember to select the 'eyes' from long stems which have borne perfect blooms – it pays dividends.

August

During the short period between first and second blooming, spray thoroughly with Buisol and Orthocide to prevent an attack of black spot and mildew on the new growths. Hoe regularly to keep down weeds. Mulch with lawn mowings. Finish buddings. Visit rose nurseries to make yourself conversant with new varieties and to make your selection of trees for the autumn.

September

Begin work on any new rose beds. Enter for, or certainly visit, the National Rose Society's autumn show. Prune summer-flowering Ramblers and tie in the new wood. Continue hoeing and keep beds free from weeds and fallen leaves. Get in supplies of farmyard manure and cover it to protect it from the rain. Potting mixture should be prepared in readiness for top-dressing pot roses next month. Pots should be washed in readiness for this operation. Now the year will begin again – a gardener's work is never done: that is the joy of it.

ROSE SOCIETIES

1. *The Local Flower Society.* There are few things more full of interest to the rose grower, whether a beginner or one of great experience, than membership of a local flower society. It may deal with many flowers, but one which will not be omitted is the rose. Seek out this society and join it. You cannot afford not to be a member there; you will meet other interested flower growers, and maybe you will find some rosarians among them. By an exchange of ideas rose lovers of all ages can learn something new; and what a kindliness there is among members of flower societies, a great willingness to help the beginner, and give him the benefit of their experience. Your local society will organize shows, and you should do your best to see that rose classes are provided in the schedule. Attend the lectures given; you will always find something of interest. Above all, remember that the success of the local society depends upon the loyal co-operation of all the members – not merely the few in office or on the committee. Without your help they cannot succeed, so see that you do your share.

2. *The National Rose Society of Great Britain,* 117 Victoria Street, London, SW1. This Society was founded in 1876, largely as a result of the efforts of that great rosarian, the Very Reverend Dean Hole. In 1857 Dean Hole had conceived the idea of holding a Grand National Rose Show, and after obtaining financial support from some of his rose-loving friends, the project was launched on 1 July 1858, when the first National Rose Show ever to be held in this country was staged in St James's Hall, Piccadilly, on the site now occupied by the Piccadilly Hotel. Entries came from widely separated parts of the country, and some ten thousand roses were on show.

Encouraged by the results of this show, others were arranged by the promoters every two or three years for the next eighteen years. Towards the end of this period a few unsuccessful shows led to the demand for a National Rose Society which would conduct and control shows and deal with other matters concerning the advancement of the rose. The demand was met, and in December 1876 the Society began what has proved to be a most successful career. For the first twenty-seven years of the Society's history Dean Hole was its President, and for twenty-five of these he had the services of the Reverend D'ombrain as Honorary Secretary. What a tremendous debt rose growers owe to these men whose untiring efforts laid the foundations of the largest and most important specialist horticultural society in the world. Membership increased from six hundred in 1901 to over four thousand in 1913. The scope of activities of the Society had been enlarged, more shows had been held, but lean years were ahead financially, and when Mr Courtney Page was appointed Secretary in 1915 the Society was some £1,500 in debt and the membership was down to one thousand.

It was largely due to his great organizing ability and his untiring zeal in the welfare of the Society that such great progress was made during the thirty-two years he held office. He saw the establishing of the Society's first Trial Ground at Hayward's Heath in 1928, where new varieties were tested for the first time under conditions which it was possible for any amateur to adopt. This very important aspect of the Society's work proved so valuable that even before the death of Mr Page in 1947 it was obvious that the Trial Ground would have to be enlarged.

In 1948 the present Trial Ground was established at the Institute of Horticulture, Oaklands, St Albans, for trying out new varieties prior to their introduction into commerce. Raisers of new roses send six plants of each variety to be tested. These rose trees come from all over the world, and large numbers are under test at one time. Each tree must remain in the Trial Ground for three years, and certificates are issued after the second or third year. After the three years all tested trees are dug up and burnt, but new plants of those which have received awards are purchased from the raisers and may be seen in the display beds of the Trial Ground.

Mr Edland, the present Secretary, has proved a most efficient and worthy successor to Mr Page and has devoted untiring energy and service to the Society he loves so well. He has seen the membership grow to over 55,000, a figure which would have appeared fantastic and astronomical at the beginning of the century.

Are you one of these 55,000 fortunate people? If not, write to the Secretary for particulars and join at once.

Recommended Kordesii Climbers for pillars and pergolas.

MAIGOLD. Golden yellow, very large, fully double. 6 ft.

ZWEIBRUCKEN. Deepest crimson. 5 ft.

KÖLN AM RHEIN. Strongly scented. Clear self pink. Large blooms in trusses, growth strong and healthy, shrub or pillar.

INDEX

INDEX

INDEX

Josephine Bruce
Margaret Mc Gredy
Sutters Gold
Piccadilly
mrs Sam mc Gredy
South Seas
Fashion

NOTES

NOTES

NOTES

NOTES

NOTES

NOTES

NOTES

NOTES

NOTES

JOSEPHINE BROCE

LADY SYLVIA

MRS SAM McGREDY